PRAISE FOR
Neil Zurcher AND One Tank Trips

"Neil Zurcher's One Tank Trips have fascinated Northern Ohioans for generations. . . . [This] book is loaded to the brim with some of his most memorable excursions." – *The Morning Journal*

"Sometimes humorous, sometimes touching, [Zurcher's] Channel 8 segments have made him something like Northeast Ohio's answer to the late Charles Kuralt." – *The Plain Dealer*

"While an Ohio travel book is nothing new, Zurcher's everyman approach to travelling is what sets it apart from the rest. . . . [He's] Ohio's foremost expert on off-beat attractions" – *Star Beacon*

"Zurcher writes as he speaks. Reading him, it's easy to think about jumping in the car with him to sample some new roadhouse and listening to his stories along the way." – *Cleveland Enterprise*

"Famous for his 20-year run as WJW TV 8's travel reporter, Zurcher is known for locating little-known, interesting, and unusual destinations within a day's drive of the Greater Cleveland area." – *Stow Sentry*

"Keep a copy in your boat, your car, whatever you happen to drive. . . . Neil Zurcher is a very talented writer." – *WERE AM Radio*

"The definitive guide for Ohio travelers." – *Chesterland News*

"If a cross-country odyssey to the Gulf Coast or Rockies isn't within your budget, Neil offers hundreds of closer-to-home destinations." – *Hudson Hub Times*

"If you can get there on a tank [of gas], Neil Zurcher has been there." – *Canton Repository*

"The variety of places Zurcher has found makes you wonder why you would ever have to vacation outside of Ohio . . . Enough to provide Ohioans with [a] most comprehensive, practical and entertaining travel guide." – *West Life*

Other books by Neil Zurcher:

More One Tank Trips

One Tank Trips Road Food

Ohio Oddities

Neil Zurcher

ONE TANK TRIPS™

AND TALES FROM THE ROAD

UPDATED 2002 2003 EDITION

GRAY & COMPANY, PUBLISHERS
CLEVELAND

With love, to two people not yet old enough to have a driver's license: my grandchildren, Allison and Bryan McCallister. May they both someday have the adventures that I have had. May they share the beauty I have seen. And may they always find something to smile about.

One Tank Trips
3rd Edition
Updated for 2002-2003

© 1995–2002 by Neil Zurcher

Gray & Company, Publishers
1588 East 40th Street
Cleveland, Ohio 44103-2302
(216) 431-2665
www.grayco.com

This guide was prepared on the basis of the authors' best knowledge at the time of publication. However, because of constantly changing conditions beyond their control, the authors disclaim any responsibility for the accuracy and completeness of the information in this guide. Users of this guide are cautioned not to place undue reliance upon the validity of the information contained herein and to use this guide at their own risk.

ISBN 1-886228-60-4
Printed in the United States of America

Contents

Northwest Ohio

Central Ohio

Southeast Ohio

Acknowledgments

I am indebted to many people who made this book possible: to Virgil Dominic, for creating the idea of One Tank Trips back in 1980 and for his many kindnesses to me; to Grant Zalba, who allowed me the freedom to wander where I wished each week; and to all of our talented videographers and editors at WJW-TV, many of whom you will meet in this book, and who travel with me each week throughout the year.

How It All Started

In 1967 when I went to work for WJW-TV, I discovered that I enjoyed doing feature stories—wandering the back roads of Ohio, seeking out the little stories that didn't ordinarily make the news. This was even before Charles Kuralt of CBS began his national wanderings. In fact, when Kuralt began his *On the Road* series in 1968, I did a parody of him in a half-hour documentary we called "R.F.D." I borrowed a huge converted Greyhound Scenicruiser bus from a friend, John Morse, chairman of the board of Morse Instruments in Hudson. John didn't like to fly, but he loved to travel and had converted this bus into a luxury home on wheels, with a movie theater on board as well as bedrooms, kitchen, and traveling office. It was magnificent! In a final scene I turned to the camera and said, "Charles Kuralt, eat your heart out."

We Americans have always been a pretty mobile society, at least in the 20th century. So in 1980 when the Mideast oil powers raised prices and threatened to cut back on petroleum supplies, Americans were hit with spiraling prices at the gasoline pump and, even worse, long lines waiting to buy the high-priced gasoline.

My boss at that time, then news director Virgil Dominic, was truly concerned that with summer coming many Ohioans would not be able to afford much of a vacation. He called me into his office to discuss an idea he had.

Virgil proposed that, because of my experience wandering the highways and byways of Ohio, I should do a week long series of reports on places that people could reach for a vacation on just one tank of gasoline. He said, "Let's call it a 'one tank trip!'"

Originally, the series was just meant to be one week long. Enough to show folks that, even with gasoline shortages, there were places to go for a holiday that summer that were fun and yet close to home. But neither Virgil nor I expected the response to the series. The phones began to ring, and the mail started to come in. People wanted more ideas on destinations.

Virgil sent me a memo telling me to put together a once-a-week segment for the rest of the spring and summer that would offer other places to go.

That autumn, when we ended the weekly segments, the mail started to flow again. Viewers didn't want the series to end. They asked for Christmas trips and activities. Again we obliged.

By the second year it was apparent that with my "one tank" formula (out and back on a tank of gasoline), I was fast running out of places to go. I went to Virgil and proposed that we extend our distance by making the destination anyplace we could reach on one tank. Even if we had to buy a second tank of gasoline to get back home, I argued, this was still, technically, a "One Tank Trip."

Virgil agreed and now, many years later, the series has become the longest-running local travel segment in television history. We travel year round to eight states and Canada and make nearly 90 trips a year. And, with the exception of special trips to Alaska and Florida, we still take just a "one tank" trip.

From My Mailbag...

Dear Neil Zurcher,

Recently you mentioned on one of your "One Tank Trips", a place To sunbathe in The nude in Tuscarawas County in The state of Ohio.
Would you be able To Tell us The whereabouts of This place? Also, is There anyplace closer To Cleveland? We would appreciate hearing from you before The weather gets much colder.

Sincerely,

Some Thoughts While Filling the Gasoline Tank

There is a very good reason why the U.S. Postal Service came up with zip codes for our mailing addresses: they had to deliver mail in Ohio.

My wife, Bonnie, who keeps track and cares about such things as where I have been, points to the problem the postal service must have had delivering mail to Ohioans before the zip code era.

There are 296 towns and villages in Ohio that share the same, exact name with another town or village in another county. And if that is not bad enough, there are 38 instances in Ohio where three towns all share the same name. Pity the poor postman who had to determine if a letter bound for Berlin, Ohio, was meant to go to the Berlin down in Williams County, or the Berlin up near Sandusky in Erie County, or the Berlin down in Holmes County where all the Amish live.

Some towns' names were so popular that they just multiplied like rabbits all over Ohio. For instance, take Avondale. There's Avondale down near the Ohio River in Belmont County, and there's Avondale over near Bellefontaine. There's Avondale near Canton in Stark County, and let's not forget the Avondale near Dayton, as well as another in Muskingham County, and the one near Cincinnati. Altogether there are six Avondales in Ohio.

And it gets worse. There are eight counties in Ohio with towns named Centerville. Now they are probably all near the center of something, which probably accounts for the name, but it makes me wonder, didn't anyone in town check the post office to see if there was another Centerville before they started painting signs at the corporate limits?

That brings us to Stringtown, Ohio, probably one of the stranger names. I can only speculate on how the name originated. Perhaps the pioneers laid out the town with bits of string to show where the various lots were. Who knows? In any event, there must have been a lot of string laid out in Ohio because Bonnie has discovered a total of 10 towns in Ohio that share the name of Stringtown.

And the postman's real nightmare was the town of Five Points.

The name probably originated from the early Native American trails that intersected and became roads and places of settlement. No fewer than *11* towns, villages, and hamlets in Ohio bear the name Five Points.

What I am leading up to here is the importance of checking addresses and directions before starting out on a One Tank Trip anywhere in Ohio, unless you like to find yourself in unexpected places and meet people who haven't the foggiest idea what you're looking for. For example, say you're heading for Boston, in Summit County, to visit the Blossom Music Center, and instead you end up at Boston down in Jefferson County. You'll probably get directions to someone's orchard if you ask anyone there how to get to Blossom.

Even if you're a seasoned Ohio traveler and think you know where everything is in the state, you may find yourself, like I did once, in the wrong Georgetown late at night, looking for a motel that doesn't exist in the Georgetown you are presently visiting. It is only then that you discover there are six Georgetowns, and the one that you want is at the other end of the state. At times like these you begin to develop a real affection for the postal service's zip codes and curse anyone who fails to include a zip code in their address.

The bottom line: use your phone. Call ahead. Get up-to-date directions, ask them to send you maps. I don't care whether you are using my travel book or someone else's, all things change with time, and if you are going to invest your family's time and money in a One Tank Trip, take a moment before you go to confirm times, places, costs, and, especially, just which Five Corners it's in.

Using This Book

When I travel Ohio, I don't think of it broken into five exact sections, northeast, northwest, southeast, southwest, and central. Rather, I loosely imagine it as a fan spreading out from Cleveland. But to organize this book it was necessary to define some geographic areas. These groupings are meant to give a general idea of where the attractions are located, to make them easier to find on a map. This may mean, for example, that the town of Millersburg, in Holmes County, is listed in a grouping of trips in Central Ohio, while Berlin, which is Millersburg's next-door neighbor, is listed under Southeast Ohio. But don't be afraid to mix and match some of the trips that are located in adjoining geographical areas.

The destinations listed in this book have been chosen by me on the basis of my own experience and from letters and phone calls I have received from "One Tank Trips" viewers over the years. None of the destinations has paid a fee to be included in this book.

Lastly, this is not intended to be a technical reference work. You won't find maps or detailed directions. Instead, this book is meant to encourage you to get out and sample some new places that might be fun, intriguing, and, hopefully, educational. Remember, half the fun of traveling is discovery. So, get out your map and plan your trip.

I offer one bit of advice. When my wife and I are on our own One Tank Trip, and I suddenly find myself at the end of a dead-end road that wasn't on the map, and she says, "You're lost, aren't you?" I always reply, "I am not lost. I just don't know exactly where I am at this moment."

Happy travels.

ONE TANK TIP #1

Call Ahead

Always, always call first. Hours, prices, and even locations are sometimes changed without notice. If you don't want to be disappointed after hours of driving, simply call first.

ONE TANK TRIPS™

AND TALES FROM THE ROAD

ALL OVER THE PLACE

1 What Is That Car?

The question I get asked most often is, "What is that car you drive?"

Sometimes before I can answer somebody will pipe up and say, "It's the car Lois Lane drove in the old Superman movies." Or, "Nahh, it's one of those kit cars, you know, like you build yourself."

Wrong on both counts. It was not the car that Lois Lane drove. She drove a Nash Rambler, which is almost twice the size of my little car. And it is not a kit car. It was a production-line car for eight years before it drove off into automobile history.

The car is a 1959 Nash Metropolitan, sometimes called the "Baby Nash." It was sold by the Nash Motor Company, which later merged with Hudson to form American Motors and even later was absorbed by the Chrysler Corporation.

The tiny Nashes were manufactured from 1954 until 1962. Probably the first truly international cars, they were built for Nash in England by the Austin Motor Company after a design by Pinin Farina of Italy. In eight years of production, fewer than 900,000 of these cars were built—compare that with the millions of cars most major car manufacturers today produce each year! There were two models: a hardtop and a convertible. Both sold for about $1,500 brand new—plus tax and title, of course.

It was a good idea—this tiny economical car—that came on the auto scene at the wrong time. In 1954 America was falling in love with big motors and even bigger tail fins. The Nash Metropolitan offered neither. It had just a 4-cylinder 1,500-cc engine that could chalk up about 30 miles to the gallon. It could carry three people in the front seat and a couple of small children in a very small rear seat.

As near as we could discover, my car started life in Florida and ended up in North Canton, Ohio, where it was stored for a number of years before I bought it in 1989. It has about 72,000 miles on it, and it still has the original motor.

Do we really take it on all those trips? The answer is "Yes . . . and

No." In the earlier years we did drive it on many of the shorter trips. But as time has gone by and the car has become a favorite with viewers, we have taken it on fewer trips in order to preserve it. When we do use it, we take quite a bit of extra footage of me driving the car and use that in segments on longer trips, or during inclement weather. The car has become a symbol of our show. In fact, at parades and personal appearances, we have had small children come up to the car and pet it. One little girl thought it was alive and gave it a hug and kiss!

A couple of times over the years we have considered replacing the little car with another vehicle, but when we polled viewers, the answer always came back, "Keep the Metro."

So we have had it painted and put new tires on it and, maybe, this spring we'll finally get around to having the motor overhauled. We'll keep driving the little red-and-white car as long as folks keep welcoming it into their living rooms via television.

Does the car have a name? We never gave it one, but Dick Goddard refers to it as the "Neil-Mobile."

IF YOU LIKE OLD VEHICLES

Ohio is rich in auto and transportation museums; here are some of my favorites. (I have listed a few more elsewhere in the book.)

Crawford Auto-Aviation Museum

THE BEST COLLECTION IN OHIO

This is probably one of the best collections in Ohio if not the whole United States. They offer some of the best examples of the earliest cars, as well as a cross-section of the cars of the 1920s and '30s and just recently have added "muscle" cars from the '50s and '60s. There is something here for every member of the family. Now if they would only add a Nash Metropolitan to the collection, it would be complete.

Crawford Auto-Aviation Museum   ☎ (216) 721-5722
10825 East Boulevard · Cleveland, Ohio
Handicapped access: yes

JUST PACKARDS

This is one of the finest privately owned museums in the state. They have taken a Packard Dealership from the 1930s and restored it—right down to the service department, where the mechanic's white coat still hangs beside his personal tool chest. They have over 45 Packards on display here from the showroom to the service department. If you like Packards, don't miss this one.

Citizens Motorcar Company   ☎ (937) 226-1917
420 S. Ludlow St. · Dayton, Ohio
Handicapped access: yes

A MOTORCYCLE MUSEUM

If you are a fan of old motorcycles, this one is for you. In this tiny college town just outside of Columbus there is a museum dedicated just to motorcycles, from the earliest models with side cars and wooden frames all the way up to some of the fastest modern bikes.

Motorcycle Hall of Fame Museum   ☎ (614) 856-2222
13515 Yarmouth Dr. · Pickerington, Ohio
Handicapped access: yes

VINTAGE BICYCLES

A local industrialist in west central Ohio who was a bicycle collector decided that his little community should have a first-rate museum. So when the owners of the famed Schwinn bicycle company decided to auction off their personal collection of vintage bicycles, he went to Chicago and bought the entire collection. Bringing it back to New Bremen, Ohio, he added it to his personal collection to create perhaps the finest bicycle museum in the country. You'll see the very first wooden bicycle, designed for troops in the Spanish-American War, and there are bicycles made to look and act like children's giant pedal cars. In this two-story museum, chances are you'll spot a look-alike for the first bicycle that you ever owned.

If you ride a bicycle or ever rode one, you'll enjoy visiting the Bicycle Museum of America.

Bicycle Museum of America   ☎ (419) 629-9249
7 W. Monroe St. (SR 274) • New Bremen, Ohio
Handicapped access: only to first floor, steps to second floor exhibits

MILITARY AIRCRAFT

The Ohio Air National Guard at Lahm Airport in Mansfield, Ohio, flies the giant C-130 Hercules cargo planes that are frequently dispatched around the world on support and humanitarian missions. While they don't advertise the fact, they do welcome visitors for tours with enough advance notice. Because of the lack of manpower for tours, they prefer larger groups, although they will accept small family groups as well.

What you will see depends on when you visit. Usually, if possible, they try to show you the inside of the C-130. They let youngsters sit in the cockpit of the aircraft and see how the huge doors are lowered to load even trucks aboard the aircraft. Most tours include the fire department staffed by the guardsmen. Kids are allowed to try on the firemen's boots and helmets, and sometimes there's a demonstration of the foam-spraying firetruck. On most tours visitors get to see the "ready room" where pilots are briefed, and meet several pilots. Each tour is a bit different and is conducted so as not to interfere with training activities. If the kids love airplanes, they will certainly like this destination, and best of all—it's free. No tours on weekends, only during duty hours on weekdays.

Ohio Air National Guard Base   ☎ (419) 521-0116 or 696-6116
179th Airlift Wing
Lahm Airport, 1947 Harrington Memorial Rd. • Mansfield, Ohio
Handicapped access: to some areas

2 Elephant Trouble

"You're gonna ride in an elephant race," said Mickey Flanagan, our assignment editor.

"A WHAT?" I replied.

"An elephant race," he said with some finality as he turned to ripping copy on the large newsroom desk.

"But Mickey," I pleaded, "you know I hate animals."

"You'll have fun," he said without looking up from his work. "It's just a promotion thing. There will be elephant keepers walking alongside controlling the animal and you just have to sit up there and go around in a circle."

So, with a great deal of reluctance, I found myself on a balmy spring day at the Cleveland Zoo. But instead of the enclosed elephant pavilion, I found myself on the large field in the center of the zoo. The zoo staff had decided not to let us ride their elephants; rather, they had brought in some privately owned elephants.

My colleagues, "Big Chuck" Schodowski and Bob "Houlihan" Wells, were already mounted on two of the smaller elephants when I arrived. A huge elephant with the unlikely name of Pansy was waiting for me.

The sight of a rather grubby elephant handler, with one leg shorter than the other, prompted some immediate speculation in my mind as to just how his leg had gotten shorter. Perhaps the elephant had eaten it!

The handler barked "DOWN!" and I was already lying on the ground when I realized he was talking to the elephant, who was ponderously squatting down on the ground.

"Just step on her leg, grab her ear, and pull yourself on top of her head," he ordered.

"Won't stepping on her leg make her upset or something?" I asked timidly.

"Nah," he grumbled at me. "She won't even feel it."

Stepping on her leg was like stepping on a rather soft rock. Pansy's ear felt like dusty leather as I tentatively grabbed and tried to jump onto her neck.

Pansy snorted softly a couple of times as I tried, time after time, to crawl, jump, or pull myself up her side and onto her neck. Finally the handler, still grumbling, walked over. As I was desperately pulling Pansy's ear and had one leg nearly onto her neck, he placed a hand on my rear end and pushed with such force that I flew up onto the neck and right off the other side.

To the laughter of the assembled crowd, I picked myself up and sheepishly walked around the front of Pansy, who, at that moment, raised her trunk and snorted right in my face, giving me the full benefit of elephant morning breath—a cross between sewer gas and the scent of skunks.

With a reeling stomach, a red face, and grim determination, I again stepped onto Pansy's spongy knee and, this time, was able to clumsily spring onto the elephant's neck.

There was no saddle, just a sort of halter that the elephant wore over her head. A large leather strap was the only thing to hang onto.

"Grip your legs just behind her ears and hang on tight to that halter," the grumbling attendant offered.

I was just trying to figure out how to pinch my legs around something that large when the attendant barked, "UP, PANSY. UP!" The elephant lurched to her feet, nearly putting me on the ground again as I grabbed the leather strap and hung on for dear life, a scream of terror bubbling up in my throat.

I suddenly found myself towering 12 feet above the ground, looking down on the hundreds of people who had gathered to watch the spectacle. It was also at this point I realized that straddling the neckbone of this elephant was like straddling a ripsaw blade.

Swaying on top of the beast, I watched as the limping keeper herded Pansy into a line with the two elephants that Big Chuck and Houlihan were atop.

We posed for pictures. I wore a nervous smile, trying to both watch the cameras and keep an eye on Pansy's handler down below to make sure he didn't decide to go off and leave me alone on top of the elephant.

Chuck Voracec, the zoo's public relations director, told the crowd that they were about to witness the first-ever elephant race at the Cleveland Zoo. I was looking around to see what elephants were going to race when, with a feeling of stark terror, I realized he was talking about the elephant I was astride, and the other two. Before I could utter even a gurgle of protest, someone raised a starter's pistol and fired a blast into the air and we were off.

We lumbered at a fast walk across the field. My limping handler seemed to be keeping up with some difficulty. I turned to see where the other two elephants were and realized that I was quite far out in front. I turned to call down to the handler to suggest we might slow down, and to my shock I found no one there.

I swiveled the other way, bringing a sharp stab of pain to the area between my legs, and to my dismay saw Pansy's handler limping and running and swearing as the elephant left him farther and farther in the dust. I was on board a runaway elephant!

In the next few moments many thoughts raced through my mind, most of them concerning death and dismemberment. I wondered, how do you stop a runaway elephant? I tried "Whoaa!" Pansy was oblivious. I pleaded with her, "Stop! Please Stop!" No good. Pansy lumbered on, heading toward the flamingo pens on the other side of the field, her speed increasing. With each stride I would fly up several inches and then slam back down on her razor-sharp back. Each time that I flew into the air I could see her massive feet below and my imagination went wild with thoughts of how I would look if I flew off and ended up squished between her toes.

Over my shoulder, Pansy's keeper and the other elephants were getting farther and farther away. I debated trying to jump from the top of the elephant, but then I would run the risk of being trampled by her back feet. Just as I was about to give up hope, Pansy suddenly stopped. I almost tumbled headfirst to the ground as her head went down and she started grazing on some flowers that were planted along the edge of the walk.

This gave her swearing, limping keeper a chance to catch up. Relief washed over me. I was almost giddy with the thought of getting off that elephant's back. The keeper placed his elephant hook in her harness and gave a command.

"UP PANSY!" he shouted.

I was expecting the animal to kneel so I could get off, not raise up on her hind feet. I suddenly found myself hanging by both hands from her harness 15 to 20 feet in the air, as the keeper yelled to me, "SMILE AND WAVE AT THE CROWD!"

I was incredulous! Here I was hanging straight down the elephant's back, clinging to the harness with such ferocity that it would have taken three men to get my hands loose, and he wanted me to wave to the crowd! In fact, when Pansy finally did kneel and they told me I could get off, he did have to pry my fingers from the harness. It took three weeks for the bruises on my inner thighs to fade.

To this day, when I walk by the elephant exhibit at the zoo I get a little nervous. I have never had the slightest desire to ride another elephant.

CLEVELAND METROPARKS ZOO AND RAINFOREST

To my knowledge they don't have elephant races anymore, but they do have a state-of-the-art rain forest that has attracted a lot of attention nationwide. The zoo is one of the finest in the state and offers a lot of things to do with the family.

Cleveland Metroparks Zoo and The RainForest ☎ (216) 661-6500
3900 Wildlife Way • Cleveland, Ohio
Handicapped access: yes

Cleveland Metroparks Zoo RainForest

THE COLUMBUS ZOO

The Columbus Zoo became nationally known under its former director, Jack Hanna, a frequent guest on television's *Tonight Show*. Even though Hanna has moved on to greener pastures, the zoo is still ranked as one of the top in the country. It is a major breeding center for lowland gorillas, cheetahs, and polar bears—all contained in a 404-acre park where the animals are kept in environmental compounds that closely resemble their natural habitats.

The Columbus Zoo   ☎ (614) 645-3400
9990 Riverside Dr. • Powell, Ohio
Handicapped access: yes

A ZOO AND HOLIDAY LIGHT FESTIVAL

The Cincinnati Zoo is considered one of the nation's top five zoos. It has one of the largest collections of rare animals in America, including 21 types of rare and endangered wild cats. They have Colossus, the largest lowland gorilla in captivity, and they also offer a "Jungle Trails" exhibit, which is a naturalized rain forest where exotic animals from Asia and Africa live.

At Christmastime, the zoo is converted into one of the best holiday light festivals in Ohio. It's a time of year when you have two reasons to visit the zoo.

Cincinnati Zoo and Botanical Garden   ☎ (800) 944-4776
3400 Vine St. • Cincinnati, Ohio
Handicapped access: yes

Cincinnati Zoo

MERMAIDS OR SEA COWS?

The Cincinnati Zoo, which already has a reputation for having an excellent holiday lighting displays, scored another coup recently when it became one of the first zoos in Ohio authorized by the U.S. Fish and Wildlife Service to give a home to injured manatees.

Thought to be mermaids by sailors who first encountered them hundreds of years ago (those sailors must have been at sea for a long, long, time), these gentle mammals have no natural predators other than man. In fact, they seem to have no fear of anything, which unfortunately brings them into close contact with man and his boat propellers. Boating accidents are the biggest single killer of manatees.

The manatees at the zoo have either been orphaned or injured and need care before they can be released back into the wild. None will be permanent residents there; in fact the mission is to get them back to their natural habitat as quickly as possible. In the meantime they have become a major attraction, pulling in long lines of visitors during the summer months. Since their pool is enclosed and climate controlled, visitors can see the huge animals, also known as "sea cows," any time of year.

Manatee Springs Exhibit   ☎ (800) 944-4776
Cincinnati Zoo and Botanical Garden
3400 Vine St. • Cincinnati, Ohio
Handicapped access: yes

THE AKRON ZOO

While not as big as some of the other zoos in the state, Akron's well-kept facility offers a close-up look at animals from all over the world. Here, too, they turn the zoo into a holiday light festival in November and December.

Akron Zoo   ☎ (330) 375-2525
500 Edgewood Ave. • Akron, Ohio
Handicapped access: yes

THE TOLEDO ZOO

Small but highly regarded, Toledo's zoo offers both year-round exhibits of animals from all over the world and a light festival at Christmastime. Many of the animal enclosures have been built to look as if the animals were in their native habitats.

Toledo Zoo   ☎ (419) 385-5751
2700 Broadway • Toledo, Ohio
Handicapped access: yes

OCEANIC ADVENTURE

It's located just across the Ohio River from downtown Cincinnati, Ohio. It's a one-of-a-kind attraction that puts you up close and personal with sharks and other sea creatures.

From the towering statue of a whale standing on its tail 40 above you to the darkened tunnel with windows that look out on the undersea world of jellyfish, you know that you are in a special place.

Just opened in 1999, the aquarium boasts tanks that contain over one million gallons of fresh- and saltwater. The building covers 100,000 square feet and contains 11,000 marine animals, including over 600 different species.

There are king penguins, and a cutaway view of the Ohio River and the species that inhabit it. There are exhibits where the kids can touch a manta ray or a shellfish. But the real attraction here is sharks! They have 50 sharks in all sizes and shapes, and they swim in a tank that you can literally walk into. A 200-foot-long seamless clear plastic tunnel lets the sharks swim over, under, and around you as you walk through their huge tank. It's quite an experience—and an opportunity to take some rather unusual family photos.

The aquarium is open daily, year round and is well worth the visit. And remember, you're just across the bridge from one of Ohio's prettiest cities and all the things to see and do there.

Newport Aquarium   ☎ (606) 491-FINS
One Aquarium Way • Newport, Kentucky
Handicapped access: yes

ONE TANK TIP #2

Save With Discounts

When booking a motel, ask for any discounts they may offer such as special corporate rates or senior citizen prices. You may be pleasantly surprised by the amount of the savings.

3 Just for Kids

Something relatively new on the museum scene is the museum just for children—where there are no "Do Not Touch" signs, no "Keep Off" warnings, or pleas to be quiet. Instead, at these museums children are encouraged to touch, feel, pull, push, and otherwise use the exhibits. Imaginations can run wild. Noisy, squeaky, squealy kinds of things add to the cacophony of hundreds of excited kids, who are not only having fun but learning valuable lessons from the many creative displays.

Living in Ohio, we are close to many top children's museums; each makes a great destination for a One Tank Trip.

Rainbow Children's Museum

A PLACE OF BRIDGES

The Cleveland Children's Museum has a wonderful exhibit that celebrates the many bridges to be found in Cleveland. Kids can go in, around, and over the display. Not only is this exhibit fun, it also teaches youngsters the importance of bridges to a city's economy. While this museum is much smaller than many similar museums, it offers a wide range of changing exhibits, as well as storytelling, toy-making, and a host of other activities to keep children entertained.

Rainbow Children's Museum   ☎ (216) 791-5437
10730 Euclid Ave. • Cleveland, Ohio
Handicapped access: yes

CINERGY CHILDREN'S MUSEUM

This children's museum opened in 1994 in a former railroad warehouse along the Ohio River. It already has more than 35,000 square feet of displays on three floors, and has options on two more floors in the giant building.

On the first floor, there are displays that will entertain and educate preschoolers—everything from a fishing exhibit with real water, where kids fish with magnets to reel in metal fish, to a place where they can roll balls down a hill and see the difference in speed when the hill is straight or curved. On the second floor, older youngsters can have fun with television special effects, learn about assembly lines, try their hands at making things, and turn giant gears by walking on a treadmill. On the third floor, there are oversized musical instruments (made by the same designer who created the floor piano that Tom Hanks danced on in the movie *Big*) and much more. I even caught several adults trying out some of the exhibits and enjoying them as much as the kids.

The Cinergy Children's Museum   ☎ (800) 733-2077
Cincinnati Museum Center
1301 Western Ave. • Cincinnati, Ohio
Handicapped access: yes

A CANADIAN FUNHOUSE

Across Lake Erie in London, Ontario, is one of the finest children's museums I have seen, located in an old elementary school. One exhibit features an igloo, where youngsters can try on a parka, climb astride a snowmobile, and put on real snowshoes. Another is dedicated to professions. Here, youngsters can dress up in real uniforms of firefighters, doctors, utility workers, or sewer workers. In fact, a mock sewer runs beneath the floor for children to explore.

In another wing of the building, children can dig in a sandpit for prehistoric fossils or dress up in dinosaur costumes. On another floor, a child-sized physics laboratory offers fun experiments for big and little kids.

London Regional Children's Museum   ☎ (519) 434-5726
21 Wharncliffe Rd. South   •   London, Ontario, Canada
Handicapped access: yes

FLY AN AIRPLANE OR SIT ON A FROG

In Flint, Michigan, there is a small but exciting children's museum that offers a real airplane for kids to climb in and on. There is also a five-foot-tall stone frog. Add to these several work—related exhibits—such as a courtroom and jail, television studio, and grocery store—where kids can play the role of adult, and you have a fun place for youngsters and parents.

Flint Children's Museum   ☎ (810) 767-5437
1602 W. 3rd St.   •   Flint, Michigan
Handicapped access: yes

THE BIGGEST IN THE MIDWEST

Indianapolis, Indiana boasts the largest children's museum in the Midwest. The museum has received wide attention for its many exciting exhibits, including a full-size, working, antique carousel that kids can ride. Some exhibits specifically address the needs of teenagers and include sophisticated fun with science, ecology, and mathematics. This is truly a museum with something for every age group.

Children's Museum of Indianapolis   ☎ (317) 334-3322
3000 N. Meridian St.   •   Indianapolis, Indiana
Handicapped access: yes

4 Regional Foods I Have Known (and Sometimes Loved)

In Cincinnati it's the chili. In Wilmot, it's an Amish wedding spread. In Chardon, it's pancakes and sauerkraut.

In many towns and regions of Ohio there is a favorite food that, though popular with the locals, just doesn't seem to catch on with the rest of us. In some cases, that's probably because we never heard of it. In other cases, it may just be that the environment gives area residents some different taste buds.

BELLYSTICKERS

In the tiny northwest Ohio town of Archbold they make a concoction known as bellystickers. These are not for the diet conscious. They're sort of like sinful Parker House rolls. In fact, they start out as fresh-baked Parker House rolls, then fresh cream and sugar are poured on top and allowed to seep through overnight. The next morning, the pan is inverted on a plate, and the bellystickers are served. If you don't care about calories, it's a wonderful way to start the day.

The Barn Restaurant and Doughbox Bakery ☎ (800) 590-9755
S.R. 2 · Archbold, Ohio
Handicapped access: yes

AN AMISH WEDDING SPREAD

The Amish areas of Ohio feature a wonderful snack concoction known as an "Amish Wedding Spread." There are several different recipes. The one I like best is a combination of peanut butter, marshmallow, and maple syrup blended and served on fresh homemade Amish bread. It is difficult to write about without salivating.

The Amish Door Restaurant ☎ (330) 359-5464
1210 Winesburg St. (U.S. 62) · Wilmot, Ohio
Handicapped access: yes

PANCAKES, SYRUP, AND . . . SAUERKRAUT

In the Northeast Ohio town of Chardon, during the annual Maple Festival you can find pancakes served with fresh-made maple syrup and . . . sauerkraut! I know, I can hear you saying, "YUKK!" already. That was my reaction, too, before I tried it. But the taste—sweet and sour and reminiscent of a Chinese egg roll—was very good. The Maple Festival is held each year on the first weekend after Easter.

Geauga County Maple Festival   ☎ (440) 286-3007
Chardon, Ohio

BRATS

They call them brats in Bucyrus. Bratwurst sausage, a German invention, has become a staple in this central Ohio town. In fact, a festival honoring the sausage is held here each year. Bratwurst is fresh pork and spices ground up and packed into links that are then grilled over charcoal fires until they split open. Slathered with mustard, sauerkraut, or horseradish sauce, they can almost be a meal by themselves. One brat maker here even has a drive-through restaurant.

W. P. I. Drive Thru Bakery and Deli   ☎ (419) 562-3332
700 N. Sandusky Ave. • Bucyrus, Ohio
Handicapped access: no

SPECIAL RECIPE LEMONADE

Lemonade is the drink of choice for many in Bellevue, Ohio. McClain's Restaurant and Old Tyme Saloon has been a fixture downtown for more than a century. The craze for lemonade started during Prohibition when the present owner's grandfather would mix up a batch of "special recipe" lemonade for thirsty regular customers. The lemonade was, allegedly, liberally laced with illegal hooch. When Prohibition ended and McClain's could legally sell booze again, customers still demanded the special recipe lemonade. Today, McClain's is an Irish pub and family restaurant known for good ribs as well as lemonade—both kinds.

McClain's Historical Restaurant   ☎ (419) 483-2727
137 E. Main St. • Bellevue, Ohio
Handicapped access: restroom not accessible

NORTHEAST OHIO

5 The Day the Circus Came to Town

"Do a feature on the circus that's in town," assignment editor Mickey Flanagan said.

"Like what?" I asked.

"Oh, you'll find something to do," he said. "You know, like try out for the trapeze act, or something."

"I think I'll do the 'or something,'" I replied as I went out the door.

The Circus Vargas was one of the last circuses still working under canvas and doing one-night stands across the Midwest. It was set up for a weekend run in a Willowick shopping center parking lot. The only problem was that the trucks carrying the tents and some of the rigging had broken down, and it was only a couple of hours to show-time. It looked like this circus was instead going to be a performance under the stars, because in the best tradition of show business, the "show must go on."

The circus public relations man was understandably a bit harried, considering that his circus was about to put on a performance in the middle of a parking lot without tents.

"The only act that can talk to you right now is Vashock!" he announced as he led me through ropes and cables and around a lion's cage.

Vashock turned out to be a small blond man with a thick Czechoslovakian accent who, I learned, did a high-wire act with his wife on a motorcycle. The motorcycle, which had no tires on it, was driven on its rims up a steel cable to a spot about forty feet over the lion's cage, at what would have been the top of the tent.

I was asking him just what the rest of the act consisted of when he interrupted to tell me that we were using up his rehearsal time and he wanted to make a couple of practice runs up the cable. "Vy dahnt you come along," he said.

I gulped and looked at the steep cable that ran to the top of a huge pole over the cage where the lions and tigers were now pacing. Videographer Gary Korb urged me on.

"Go ahead!" Korb said. "You know they want some reporter involvement in these stories."

"I don't think that looks too safe," I replied, again tilting my head back to see how far up the cable ran.

"You don't think he'd let you do anything dangerous," Gary said. "He'll probably just take you up a few feet and then come right back down."

Vashock stood there smiling, saying, "Yah, Yah. Ve gif you short ride."

The motorcycle was already sitting on the wire, atop a wooden stand, about six feet off the ground. Beneath it, attached to the motorcycle, was a steel trapeze with straps on each side. I sat down on the trapeze and Vashock immediately began strapping my hands to the side bars.

"Why are you doing this ?" I asked, nervously.

"Because I dahn't want you to be scared and jump off," he replied as he climbed onto the motorcycle above me and kick-started it. Whatever I said in reply was lost in the roar of the motorcycle. We started to move. I grabbed the steel bars with an iron grip as we went up, and up, and up. I finally opened my eyes and looked down. Below me, looking directly up at me was the largest lion I have ever seen in my life, and his mouth was open, teeth gleaming!

Just then the motorcycle shut off and we sat there gently swaying back and forth, balanced on a single, silvery steel cable 40 feet over the lions and the blacktop parking lot.

"How you lak this?" Vashock shouted down to me.

I was too frightened to answer. I managed to look at him and open my mouth, but not a word would come out. Finally I was able to work my lips into a slight grimace, which Vashock immediately mistook for a smile of encouragement.

"Maybe we do a couple of loop-loops!" he shouted down to me as he started to swing the motorcycle in a crazy side-to-side motion. My weight was the only thing that was keeping the cycle on the wire!

"D-D-D-DOWN!" I finally managed to get out.

"Down?" Vashock said perplexed.

"Yes, take me DOWN!" I shouted. "I forgot something on the ground."

"Okeydokey," Vashock answered as he fired up the motorcycle, and we started coasting backwards, back towards the ground.

When we were finally back down and my hands had been pried from the trapeze bar, Vashock asked me, "Vot did you forget?"

"My courage," I truthfully replied. "Why did you take me all the way to the top?"

He smiled, a bit sheepishly.

"Mine rigging is still on the truck that is not here," he explained, "and I had to use someone else's cables and mine wife is pregnant and I didn't want her on board when I tested the cables. I think, if it don't break with you on board trapeze, it is safe for her to do the show."

The traveling circus may almost be just a memory, but there are lots of family fun places still left here in northern Ohio—particularly amusement parks, from century-old Geauga Lake, with its modern-day theme park attractions, to a place that has remained unchanged for generations: Memphis Kiddie Park.

MEMPHIS KIDDIE PARK

If you were a youngster growing up in the 1950s on the west side of Cleveland, chances are you probably spent some of your summer days at Memphis Kiddie Park in Brooklyn. The good news is that absolutely nothing has changed there in over 50 years. The very same rides, the tiny merry-go-round, mini–roller coaster, little Ferris wheel, and kiddie train that passes Snow White and the seven concrete dwarfs are all just as they were back in 1950, though perhaps a different color.

Memphis Kiddie Park   ☎ (216) 941-5995
10340 Memphis Ave. • Brooklyn, Ohio
Handicapped access: yes

SIX FLAGS WORLDS OF ADVENTURE

Six Flags and the former SeaWorld Ohio have united to create Six Flags Worlds of Adventure, a 750-acre three-in-one amusement center. It's a thrill park, educational marine life park, and a family water park all in one. It offers rides and attractions ranging from thrill rides—like their ten roller coasters—to shows including one with their new killer whale, Shouka. The water park, Hurricane Harbor, features 21 water slides.

Six Flags Worlds of Adventure   ☎ (330) 562-7131
1060 Aurora Rd. • Aurora, Ohio
Handicapped access: yes

Six Flags Worlds of Adventure

AMUSEMENT PARK BOOKS

Euclid Beach Park now exists only in spirit—in the nostalgic thoughts of the folks who grew up spending summers riding the rides and enjoying the lakefront views. But a local publishing company has saved some of the memories in a pictorial history of the park (they have one on Conneaut Lake, too). They are books full of memories.

Amusement Park Books   ☎ (440) 331-6429
20925 Mastick Rd. • Fairview Park, Ohio

EUCLID BEACH, THE CATALOG

Though Euclid Beach Park may be gone, the family that once operated it is still in business—producing memories of the park. The Humphrey Company still makes the famous popcorn balls and taffy that were Euclid Beach trademarks. They sell gift boxes by mail and in area gift stores.

No store, mail order only. For a catalog, write to:

The Humphrey Company   ☎ (800) 486-3739
20810 Miles Pkwy • Warrensville Hts., Ohio

6 Hamburgers and Ice-Cream Cones

We all know that there is no ham in hamburger, but there almost was. Two brothers, Charles and Frank Menches, from Canton, Ohio, were running a food tent at the Erie County Fair in Hamburg, New York, in 1885. Their specialties were a freshly ground sausage sandwich, orange cider, oysters, and cigars. They would use fresh pork, add their own ingredients and spices to it, and then press it into a patty shape and fry it on a grill for hungry fair-goers.

The sausage sandwiches sold well, but fate intervened. That summer was so hot that butchers did not dare slaughter any pigs, so there was a sausage shortage. Frank went searching local suppliers and could only come up with ground beef. They decided to try it, but it didn't taste quite right, so they tried other seasonings—coffee, brown sugar, and other things. They liked the taste. More importantly, their customers loved it, and when one asked what they called the sandwich, Frank Menches, looking at the name of the town—"Hamburg"—on a nearby banner, replied, "It's a Hamburger!"

And so was born the sandwich that would spawn a million imitations and become the symbol of American food.

But history was not done with the Menches brothers. At the 1904 St. Louis World's Fair, they were peddling their "hamburgers" and selling homemade ice cream served on some fresh waffles. Reportedly, a young girl who didn't want to sit down to eat her ice cream asked for some way to take it with her. One of the Menches brothers had an inspiration: he grabbed a fresh waffle from the waffle maker, took one of this tent pegs, wrapped the waffle around it to make a cone, and then placed the ice cream inside it.

The ice-cream cone was born.

Today, the Menches brothers' great-great-grandchildren have restaurants in Green and Akron, where they serve both the original-recipe hamburgers, made with coffee, brown sugar, and a "secret ingredient," and homemade waffle ice-cream cones.

Menches Brothers Original Hamburgers, 1885 ☎ (330) 896-2288
3700 Massillon Rd., Suite 130 • Green, Ohio
Handicapped access: yes

Menches Brothers Original Hamburgers, 1885 ☎ (330) 375-1717
Canal Park, 300 S. Main St. • Akron, Ohio
Handicapped access: yes

A PARK FOR ALL PEOPLE

The Stark County Park District has attempted to make Sippo Lake a park that everyone—old, young, middle-aged, and the physically challenged—can enjoy. For openers, there is the fishing pier, the largest inland fishing pier in Ohio. The picnic area is built in the shape of a pirate ship on the tree-shaded shore of the lake.

You can rent a rowboat for a dollar an hour, and small motor boats are equally inexpensive. In the marina you'll find one of the largest fishing tackle collections in the state.

For the youngsters there is a nature center, where abandoned and injured animals are cared for and nursed back to health, as well as an outstanding display of stuffed animals from around the world.

Perception Park, just across the lake, is dedicated to physically challenged people. There is an all-people's paved path that leads to the lake, with sturdy park benches along the edge of the path. All picnic tables are wheelchair accessible, as are the barbecue grills. There is a ramp that leads to a gazebo at the edge of the lake. All restrooms are also accessible to the handicapped. Best of all, admission to the park is free.

Sippo Lake Park   ☎ (330) 477-3552
Stark County Park District
5300 Tyner Ave., N.W. • Canton, Ohio
Handicapped access: yes

HOME OF THE FIRST LADIES

Just about every president of the United States has a library or museum somewhere named for him. But what about the power behind all these famous men—the first ladies of America? These women, with the exception of Eleanor Roosevelt and Jackie Kennedy, have remained in the shadow of their famous husbands and been footnotes to history.

That has changed with the opening of the National First Ladies' Library, in the Canton home of the wife of the 25th president. Ida Saxton McKinley lived in this South Market Street home before and after she married William McKinley. Today, the historic home has been turned into a beautiful tribute to all first ladies.

The museum displays pictures and personal possessions of many of the women. The library contains an eclectic assortment of books, about first ladies, many of them out of print. An internet site organizes all the information that can be found around the country about the women who served as first ladies. Less than a year old, the operation is already expanding to a nearby bank building that will serve as a more permanent site for the library, while the Saxton-McKinley Home will remain a historical museum.

Tours of the Saxton-McKinley home are available Tuesday through Saturday by reservation only.

National First Ladies' Library / Ida Saxton McKinley Home
☎ (330) 452-0876
331 S. Market Ave. • Canton, Ohio
Handicapped access: yes

National First Ladies' Llibrary

CLASSIC CARS ON DISPLAY

This museum offers a look not only at the cars of the early part of this century, but also at the restoration work on some of the great old classics that are being readied for display. Included in the collection is a police car from the 1930s that has bullet-proof glass. The museum is small but will interest anyone interested in old cars.

Canton Classic Car Museum   ☎ (330) 455-3603
Market Ave. at 6th St. SW • Canton, Ohio
Handicapped access: yes

7 Read the Fine Print

"Remember, you have a speech tomorrow in Warren, Ohio," my wife Bonnie reminded me.

"On a Monday morning?" I asked.

"Check the calendar," she replied as she walked out of the room.

I walked to the desk, and there it was circled on my calendar: "March 19, 1992, Packard Music Hall, Warren, Ohio, 9:00 a.m. Speech."

The alarm clock rang at six o'clock on Monday morning. Outside, a late winter snow was falling, and early radio newscasts were warning motorists to prepare for a long drive to work. I drove across the Ohio Turnpike wondering if the weather would affect the turnout at the speech I was to make. Spun-out trucks dotted the turnpike median strip, and it was a white-knuckle trip every mile of the way.

At 8:45 a.m. I reached the Packard Music Hall parking lot. It was empty. My tire tracks in the fresh snow were the only ones. I drove to the rear of the building. No cars there. Perhaps I was early. I waited.

Fifteen minutes later, when the speech was to have started, I was still the only one in the parking lot. I picked up my cellular phone and called Kevin Salyer at TV-8, who had set up the speech.

"Kevin," I said, with some sarcasm, "I just drove through a snowstorm to Warren, Ohio, and no one is here."

"Let me check the invitation," he replied. "I'll be right back."

There was a short pause, and then he came back on the phone.

"Do you have the copy of the invitation I gave you?" he asked, a sarcastic tinge in *his* voice.

"Certainly!" I replied, "It's right here on the seat beside me."

"Read the date to me," he said.

"Just like I told you," I began, "March 19, 9:00 a.m."

"No," he said, "the WHOLE date."

I looked at the letter again and read, "March 19, 1993." I had arrived at the speech too early. One year too early.

A WARREN TRADITION

Just about anyone who has ever lived in Warren, or even just stopped by for a visit, has had at least one hot dog at this downtown

Warren institution. Here they have a secret, closely guarded sauce that they use on the hot dogs, and they go through hundreds of them every day. Many fans buy the dogs by the bagful.

The Hot Dog Shoppe   ☎ (330) 395-7057
740 W. Market St. • Warren, Ohio
Handicapped access: step into restaurant

WHERE CELEBRITIES STAY AND PLAY

In Warren, it's the Avalon Inn that attracts both local folks and the rich and famous who visit here. A fine restaurant, lovely rooms, and a championship golf course with beautiful grounds make this a great getaway for families. Some of the biggest names in golf have played this course.

The Avalon Inn   ☎ (330) 856-1900
9519 E. Market St. • Warren, Ohio
Handicapped access: yes

THE GHOSTS OF THE PAST

Warren offers an unusual Halloween tradition. Each October, the Fine Arts Council gets actors to portray famous residents who once lived along "Millionaires' Row." In the evening, as you walk along the street, "ghosts" of these residents drift by to tell stories of the grief and scandal they faced. Tours leave from the First Presbyterian Church, located at 256 Mahoning Avenue, and include a visit to the Pioneer Cemetery.

Of course celebrating Halloween is not the only thing the Fine Arts Council does for the city. Write or call them for a current schedule of events.

Fine Arts Council of Trumbull County   ☎ (330) 399-1212
P.O. Box 48 • Warren, Ohio
Handicapped access: yes

MILITARY TANKS, TRUCKS, AND MORE

Henry Venetta didn't serve in World War II, but his relatives' participation in the D-Day invasion touched off a lifelong hobby for

Henry, and it has produced a museum. Henry is a heavy-equipment operator, so it wasn't much of a leap for him to become interested in tanks from the World War II period. So far he has used his expertise to buy and completely restore a total of 26 World War II tanks, trucks, and large weapons. For his museum, he has taken over an old tennis club: where tennis balls once flew, huge olive-drab tanks now sit, looking as though the soldiers that manned them have just gone out for lunch. Some of the vehicles are complete down to the cans of C-rations in a compartment near where the ammunition was stored.

Henry has collected weapons used in both theaters of the war, the Atlantic and the Pacific. There is a rare motor scooter used by airborne troops who dropped the little scooter into Normandy for use on the French roads. There is also the largest truck made during World War II, used for tank repair and retrieval.

This is a private museum, so it is wise to call before visiting for hours and admission policies. Henry has a special affection for veterans' groups and has been known to put the coffeepot on when veterans who once manned these tanks are visiting.

World War II Military Vehicle Museum   ☎ (330) 534-8125
5959 W. Liberty St. • Hubbard, Ohio
Handicapped access: ramps in the building

MORE INFORMATION

Check for maps, brochures, and other ideas if you're planning a visit to Trumbull County by calling or writing:

Trumbull County Convention and Visitors Bureau   ☎ (800) 672-9555
650 Youngstown-Warren Rd. • Niles, Ohio
Handicapped access: yes

ONE TANK TIP #3

Troop on in for a Map

If you need a map check state police posts along most major highways. They usually have state maps and usually they are free.

8 A School's Home Is Its Castle

Strangers wandering into the Alliance City School District's office often do a double take. The main hall is guarded by a life-size suit of armor. In the rotunda is a crystal chandelier, a duplicate of one presented years ago to the Shah of Iran. There are secret passages, a swimming pool, and a bowling alley, as well as a wine cellar and a ballroom.

Welcome to Glamorgan Castle, and yes, it really is the office of the Alliance City Schools.

The Castle was built in 1904 as a private residence for Alliance industrialist Colonel William Henry Morgan. It cost $400,000 and took five years to build. The stone walls above the ground are a minimum of 13 inches thick.

Glamorgan Castle

The property had many owners down through the years. It served as the home of the local Elks lodge, and then as corporate headquarters for the Alliance Machine Company. In 1973, through a series of federal grants, the Castle and 20 acres of land were turned over to the Alliance Schools.

Tours can be arranged by calling the school district office during the school year. Group tours can sometimes be arranged for other times.

Glamorgan Castle   ☎ (330) 821-2100
200 Glamorgan St. • Alliance, Ohio
Handicapped access: steps in building

GRINDERS FOR LUNCH

If you are wondering what the heck a grinder is, it's like a submarine sandwich. Lots of meat, cheese, and veggies served on a chewy roll. But here they serve much more—everything from Cajun Steak to Santa Fe Chicken. And then there are the desserts. Specialties are the banana split pie and the "choc-o-holic" brownie sundae.

Grinders Above and Beyond   ☎ (330) 821-6665
1820 W. State St. • Alliance, Ohio
Handicapped access: yes

LIBRARY IN A MALL

If you have family members who hate to shop, take them along to the Carnation Mall in Alliance, where you'll find one of the only public libraries located in a shopping mall. They can browse, relax in the reading room, or check out books while the rest of the family goes shopping. Open 9–9 Mon–Thu; 9–5:30 Fri–Sat.

Rodman Public Library   ☎ (330) 821-1313
Carnation Mall
2500 W. State St. • Alliance, Ohio
Handicapped access: yes

SLEEP AND SHOP

You can spend the night in a shopping mall here in Alliance, Ohio. The Comfort Inn anchors one end of the Carnation Shopping Mall. The hotel offers many amenities: whirlpool baths in some rooms, an indoor swimming pool, an exercise room, and packages that include tickets to the movie theaters just off the lobby or dinner in your room served by a restaurant in the mall.

Comfort Inn   ☎ (800) 948-5555 reservations; (330) 821-5555 local
Carnation Mall, 2500 W. State St. • Alliance, Ohio
Handicapped access: yes

WHERE THE BUFFALO ROAM

One of the larger privately owned buffalo, or bison, herds in Ohio is located not far from Alliance. The owner offers tours of the ranch where he raises the animals for meat and hides. Winter seems to be a good time to visit and see the young calves cavorting in the fields. The meat of the bison is becoming popular with folks who are watching their fat intake. Nutritionists say that bison meat is less fatty than beef or even turkey. Tours by reservation.

1880 Buffalo Ranch ☎ (330) 877-6494
2545 Pontius St., N.E. • Hartville, Ohio
Handicapped access: gravel and dirt paths to barn and fields

A HEALTHY PLACE TO EAT

While the owners here didn't set out to specialize in health-conscious meals, they decided not to deep-fry foods but broil them instead because that tastes better. The result has been good food that is also healthy, and this small restaurant attracts a lot of people for its medium-priced meals. The restaurant is open seven days a week.

Taster's Choice Café ☎ (330) 821-6666
1908 S. Union Ave. • Alliance, Ohio
Handicapped access: yes

AN OLD-FASHIONED BANANA SPLIT

This candy store, soda fountain, and sandwich shop has been a Stark County institution for generations. Heggy's Candies are famous in many parts of the state, but local folks also head for Heggy's for fountain treats like old-fashioned banana splits made with vanilla, chocolate, and strawberry ice cream and mounded with whipped cream and cherries. It's the kind of place where you think about putting off that diet you were going to start today until tomorrow.

Heggy's Candies ☎ (330) 821-2051
1306 W. State St. • Alliance, Ohio
Handicapped access: yes

From My Mailbag...

Neil Zurcher:

My family and I took that trip you told about to Elmira, New York. We ran out of gas on the way there and had to call a Tow Truck to get going again. You ruined our afternoon. I am enclosing the bill for the Tow Truck and the gasoline to get back home. Please remit by return mail.

--Lost in New York

9 Ohio's Own Flying Saucer

How many states can claim to have a flying saucer as a tourist attraction? For nearly 40 years motorists traveling along U.S. Route 20 in Northeast Ohio did the proverbial double take on entering the small town of Ashtabula. A saucer 51 feet in diameter, with a clear bubble cockpit on the top, perched atop a 10-foot-tall column right where routes 11, 46 and 20 all came together. In its last days it looked as if it had been abandoned for many years, as though some alien space pilot had landed to sample the pleasures of downtown Ashtabula long ago and never returned.

The real story was less romantic. The "saucer" was built by Ashtabula resident Ray Keyes in 1966 as a Gas-n-Go gasoline station. Its futuristic design was intended to capitalize on the space and UFO craze that was then sweeping the country. The perimeter of the saucer was lined with 500 blinking, pulsating lights to attract customers. At Christmastime, Keyes used to prop a mannequin of Santa Claus in the cockpit.

Sometimes customers were heard to ask the attendant if Captain Kirk of the Starship Enterprise was aboard.

But eventually new traffic patterns caused by interstate highways and shopping malls, and ecological concerns about buried gasoline tanks, made turning a profit too hard for such small, independent gasoline stations, and Ashtabula's Gas-n-Go shut down.

For a long time there was talk of a new business, perhaps a tourist information center, taking over the building, but nothing happened. The end came just after the turn of the new century when a wrecking crew moved in to carefully dismantle the saucer and truck it away. Its new home is to be the Crawford Auto-Aviation Museum in Cleveland, where it may serve as a reminder that Ashtabula, Ohio, was once the home of Ohio's only gas-pumping flying saucer.

COVERED BRIDGE CAPITAL

The people of this county not only preserve their old covered bridges, they appreciate them so much they are building new ones! These bridges are economical and scenic as well as a tourist attraction. A covered bridge festival is held each autumn to celebrate the

14 bridges that now exist in Ohio's largest county. And more bridges will be completed soon. Maps of the bridges are available year round from the festival headquarters in Jefferson.

Covered Bridge Festival ☎ (440) 576-3769
25 W. Jefferson St. • Jefferson, Ohio
Handicapped access: yes

RAILROAD RIDE

There is a working railroad here in the county seat of Ashtabula County. On weekends, it also hauls tourists in antique passenger cars over a short line that runs through forests and swamps and near the town.

A C & J Railroad Company ☎ (440) 576-6346
160 E. Walnut St. • Jefferson, Ohio
Handicapped access: steps into railroad cars

CUT YOUR OWN CHRISTMAS TREES

Ashtabula offers some of the larger Christmas tree plantations in the state. Two of them provide a unique way to get your annual treat: ride a horse-drawn wagon back into the fields, cut your own tree, throw it on the wagon, and haul it back to the office. It makes a great family holiday tradition. Usually open from late November/early December until Christmas.

Manners Pine Tree Lodge ☎ (440) 294-2444
780 Dodgeville Rd. • Jefferson, Ohio
Handicapped access: ramps to wagon

Henson's Hideaway Tree Farm and Nursery ☎ (440) 294-2292
1155 Brockway Rd. • Rome, Ohio
Handicapped access: yes

GO PROSPECTING

You can actually pan for diamonds and other precious stones here in Ashtabula County. The NOEMA Gem Mine is a unique business that lets you take a bucket and sift through "tailings" that they have purchased from mines around the world. Any precious or semiprecious stones are yours to keep. A jewelry business on site can mount any stone you find. While you may not find the Hope Diamond, they claim that most people do find some kind of semi-precious stone that can be turned into a necklace or bracelet.

NOEMA Gemstone Mine   ☎ (440) 275-3211
1788 Mill St. · Austinburg, Ohio
Handicapped access: gravel driveway

A BABY-BUGGY MUSEUM

It's perhaps the only museum of its kind in the world. The Perambulator Museum started out as a hobby for two sisters and has now grown into a tourist attraction. Included in the collection is the Victorian perambulator used in the movie, *Gone With the Wind*. They also have early sleds and other conveyances used to transport children in the last two or three centuries. Many of the pieces on display are one of a kind.

The Victorian Perambulator Museum of Jefferson   ☎ (440) 576-9588
26 E. Cedar St.
Off Rte. 46 · Jefferson, Ohio
Handicapped access: steps into house, narrow doorways

HISTORIC FRITTERS

Back in 1798, when this tavern was built, its cooks started making corn fritters for the dining room guests and now, nearly two hundred years later, they are still using the same recipe.

The famous landmark restaurant also serves many other tasty, made-from-scratch items that keep their customers coming back again and again.

The Old Tavern at Unionville   ☎ (800) 782-8376
7935 S. Ridge Rd. (Rte. 84) · Unionville, Ohio
Handicapped access: yes

10 Wrong-Way River

"Hold it right there!" videographer Bill West shouted to me.

I was holding "it"—a canoe—by paddling frantically against the current in the Black Fork River here in Loudonville.

"Okay!" West shouted. "Paddle by me again and this time, SMILE!"

I gritted my teeth and sloshed the cold springtime water with my paddle. The current was so strong that I really had little to do other than keep the boat upright and steer it near the center of the river. I glided by West's photography station on the bank and once again started paddling hard against the current to stop the boat.

"Take it back up river again!" West called.

Once more I pushed and pulled on the paddle, battling the current as the canoe bucked and twisted in the water. Finally, I worked my way about 200 feet upstream where I cautiously turned the canoe and grabbed onto an overhead tree limb to keep from scooting downstream again.

"You know, that water is cold," I offered to West as he set up his camera in a different location.

"Just remember to smile as you go by me and we'll be done here," he prodded me.

On West's signal I started paddling downstream again, trying to look like I did this every day of the week and was an old hand at canoeing.

But just as I passed West's position I felt the canoe rock. I grabbed the sides and hung on for dear life.

West shouted at me, "Aww, you screwed it up again! Take it back upstream."

The boat seemed to settle down, and I reached for the paddle that I had dropped in the middle of the canoe. Then it happened.

My weight caused the boat to rock to the right, nearly overturning. I flung my weight to the opposite side, overreacting and overcorrecting, and the canoe started rocking the other way so violently that I knew I was going into the river.

I dropped the paddle and clawed at my hip pocket, flinging my wallet towards shore as I tried, at the same time, to tear off my non-waterproof watch and hurl it to shore. My arm was in midair when I went upside down into the cold river. Since the river is only about three feet deep in most areas, I hit bottom immediately and shot back to the surface.

"*&*%$#%^&," I shouted as I also spewed a mouthful of brown river water into the air. I regained my feet on the slippery river bottom and started to wade towards shore just in time to see my wallet starting to sink beneath the surface. There was no choice but to dive for it. I managed to retrieve it, and also my hat, which had floated off my head in the capsizing.

Bill West stood on the bank with a funny smile on his face and said, "I didn't have the camera running. If you did that intentionally we'll have to do it over."

Between curses, I informed him that it was NOT intentional and we would NOT do it again. Frankly, I was grateful that there was no footage of the embarrassing accident and that no one besides West had seen it.

While West went off to shoot some more proficient canoers, I slopped my way back to the parking lot. It had turned into a sunny day, and I noticed that the parking lot was empty, save one woman at the other end. I tossed my wallet onto the trunk of our car. I spread out the sodden bills and cards. I peeled off my socks and shoes and laid them on the trunk to dry, and was just unbuttoning my shirt, when I noticed the woman was taking pictures of me.

Jo Lemon of the Ashland newspaper had heard we were in the area and had come to interview me. The following week, there I was in all my wet and bedraggled glory, on the front page of the newspaper, wringing out my socks. It gave her readers a firsthand look at the "glamour" of television.

A footnote: Dick Schrafrath, the former Cleveland Browns star, who operated the canoe livery where we were doing the taping, saw the segment, and the next time I came asking for a canoe to use in a story, he offered me one with outrigger pontoons—sort of a canoe with training wheels!

Despite my problems, I found that the Loudonville area offers many fun things to do for the family.

Downtown Loudonville Canoe Livery ☎ (888) 226-6356
424 W. Main St. • Loudonville, Ohio
Handicapped access: ramp to water

MOHICAN STATE PARK

This beautiful state park offers a lodge tucked away far from highways and towns. Hollywood types like Alan Alda and Paul Newman have stayed here more than once. Besides a modern lodge, cabins, camping, and seclusion, the park offers lakes with fishing, some great wooded hiking trails, and Ohio's Veterans' Memorial Chapel.

Mohican State Park ☎ (419) 994-4290
3116 State Rte. 3 · Loudonville, Ohio
Handicapped access: yes, except cabins

Mohican Lodge Resort and Conference Center ☎ (419) 938-5411
County Rd. 3006 (off McCurdy Rd., north of SR 97) · Perrysville, Ohio
Handicapped access: yes

Mohican State Park Lodge

OUTSIDE THE PARK

If you can't get into the lodge and want something better than a tent, try this motel chain near the interstate highway. It's a relatively new building that offers whirlpool baths in some suites, breakfast included, and a swimming pool—for a surprisingly low price.

Comfort Inn ☎ (419) 886-4000
I-71 at S.R. 97
855 Comfort Plaza Dr. · Bellville, Ohio
Handicapped access: yes

THINGS TO DO

There are all the usual tourist things to do here. One of the long-time attractions is Mohican Family Fun Center. They have go-karts, horseback riding, and canoe and float trips. They are located just a short distance from Mohican State Park.

Mohican Canoe Livery & Fun Center   ☎ (800) 662-2663
Rte. 3 (1 mile south of Loudonville) · Loudonville, Ohio
Handicapped access: yes to some attractions

From My Mailbag...

Mr. Zurcher,

My girlfriend and I went to that non-electric bed-and-breakfast you wrote about. When we got there we found they didn't have any electric lights or indoor toilets. We had a terrible time. You should not tell about these places unless you explain that non-electric means no lights!!

--Lights out in New Philadelphia

11 Ohio's Presidential Trail: William McKinley

William McKinley, our 25th president, was born in Niles, Ohio, and spent most of his adult life in Canton. He was a major in the Civil War, served as a congressman from Ohio, and served three terms as governor of Ohio. He had been elected to his second term as president of the United States when he was assassinated while speaking in Buffalo, New York, in 1901. He was brought back to Canton, and today his tomb dominates the city skyline. At the time of his death he was the third U.S. president in 36 years to be assassinated, after Abraham Lincoln in 1865 and James A. Garfield in 1881.

McKinley Museum

The tomb sits on a bluff overlooking a park and the building that houses the McKinley Museum of History, Science and Industry. This is a wonderful museum that offers a glimpse not only into the life of William McKinley, but also into the industries and national firms that were either founded or have grown in Canton and have had an impact on our way of life. The newest addition is a hands-on discovery museum for youngsters of all ages that includes a life-size animated dinosaur, an electrical display that will really stand your hair on end, and a host of other interesting things for kids to see and do.

McKinley Museum & National Memorial ☎ (330) 455-7043
800 McKinley Monument Dr., N.W. • Canton, Ohio
Handicapped access: yes

FRIED SPINACH LEAVES

That's just one of the unusual dishes offered at this family restaurant on Lincoln Way in Massillon. They are also famous for their sticky buns, which servers keep offering as you eat your meal here. Lots of made-from-scratch dishes and wonderful desserts. Especially their strawberry pie!

Open seven days.

D. D. Stutz Restaurant   ☎ (330) 477-2525
4508 Lincoln Way • Massillon, Ohio
Handicapped access: yes

ONE OF MY FAVORITE BOOKSTORES

This newsstand has been a downtown Canton fixture for decades. Just about any magazine published can be found on the shelves, especially those dealing with sports and hobbies. They also have a well-stocked bookstore here and offer many volumes at bargain prices. I was especially happy to see the number of books they carry by Ohio authors, some published locally and very hard to find.

The News Depot   ☎ (330) 454-4441
207 N. Market St. • Canton, Ohio
Handicapped access: yes

THE FOOTBALL HALL OF FAME

Canton is the birthplace of professional football and the home of the Pro Football Hall of Fame. Busts of football heroes and artifacts from past years of gridiron glory are on display; you can also match wits with football experts via interactive exhibits. The hall adds new members each August, and the ceremonies are held on the lawn in front of the football shrine. There is also a gift shop.

Pro Football Hall of Fame   ☎ (330) 456-8207
2121 George Halas Dr. • Canton, Ohio
Handicapped access: yes

THE FUMBLEBALL HALL OF FAME

There really is such a game and such a place. It is also right here in Canton. Fumbleball is like softball and usually played by persons over the age of 35. There are only two leagues in the country, one in Canton, where a hall of fame has been established to honor its members.

Fumbleball Hall of Fame   ☎ (330) 453-1552
Greater Canton Amateur Sports Hall of Fame
1414 Market Ave., N. · Canton, Ohio
Handicapped access: no

A VACUUM CLEANER MUSEUM

The folks who make the Hoover Vacuum Cleaner have turned their founder's boyhood home in North Canton into a museum for their machine. Included in the displays are cleaning devices that go back hundreds of years, as well as early Hoover models. It's an interesting stop, especially on a rainy day.

Hoover Historical Center   ☎ (330) 499-0287
1875 Easton St. · North Canton, Ohio
Handicapped access: steps to upper floors

A REAL OLD-FASHIONED ICE-CREAM PARLOR

During the Football Hall of Fame festivities each year, you can usually find some football greats dropping into this Canton landmark, which has stood in the same spot for nearly 70 years. You might even find initials from the 1930s carved in some of the tables.

What they serve here is real homemade ice cream, made the same way for nearly seven decades. The big seller is a dish made with three-quarters of a pound of vanilla ice cream, homemade chocolate syrup, and fresh-roasted pecans, all blended together and topped with a mound of whipped cream. It's called a "Bittner." No one seems quite sure how the name originated. It's believed that it was named for an early employee who developed the treat, which is served in a soda glass with a spoon.

Taggart's Ice Cream   ☎ (330) 452-6844
1401 Fulton Rd., N.W. · Canton, Ohio
Handicapped access: yes

12 My Adventures with Craig

When my son, Craig, was about four years old I had an emergency. My wife had left for work, I was slated to make a One Tank Trip that day, and our baby-sitter called to say she was sick.

What was I going to do with my four-year-old son?

I took him with me.

I called videographer Ralph Tarsitano, whom we call "Tarts," explained my problem, and asked if he would object to Craig riding along with us. (I didn't bother to clear it with WJW-TV.)

Everything went fine on the shoot. Craig seemed to enjoy the attention he was getting by being the youngest member of a TV crew. It was Christmastime, and he was fascinated by the lights, the decorated store windows, and all the excitement.

A department store Santa Claus was sitting in a window talking to youngsters. Tarts had watched several kids press their noses against the window to watch, but by the time he got the camera in position the kids had wandered off. He pointed to Craig.

"Put him over by the window and let me get a shot of him watching Santa," he said.

I wasn't too sure.

"Uhhh, Tarts," I began, "I forgot to get clearance to bring Craig along."

"Nobody's gonna recognize him back at the station," Tarsitano replied as he motioned Craig into position. "Don't worry about it."

When Craig looked through the window his four-year-old eyes got as wide as pie plates as he beheld Santa Claus talking to the other youngsters.

I used the shot—just one of many in a pretty piece about Christmas coming to Chagrin Falls. A day later I was summoned to then-news director Phyllis Quail's office.

"Was that your son Craig on that Christmas piece last night?" Phyllis asked.

I admitted that it was, but before I could begin my assurances that it was an emergency and that it would not happen again, she interrupted me.

"That was cute," she said. "You ought to take him with you more often. Our viewers like to see that we have families just like them."

I hastily agreed with her and said that, when possible, I would consider doing just that. At the same time I was mentally calculating how much I could also save in baby-sitting fees on days I traveled.

So, off and on, for the next 10 years, especially during school holidays and the summer, Craig became my partner on One Tank Trips. During those years he got to steer a real paddle-wheel boat down the Ohio River and ride in the fireman's seat of a steam-powered locomotive. He rode a jet-boat up the Niagara gorge. He took elephant rides and petted baby tigers. He watched the sun rise and set in different states. In short, he got to do things that many youngsters might only fantasize about.

But Craig never caught a fish.

I must confess I am not a fisherman, and throughout Craig's life I have taken him fishing probably fewer than a half-dozen times. When we visited the new Geneva State Park in Geneva-on-the-Lake a couple of years ago and a charter captain offered to take us where the really big fish were biting, we jumped at the chance.

The boat was only about 19 feet long, and as we headed out into the lake, some four- to six-foot waves were beginning to roll. We bobbed around like a cork in a barrel as we pushed a mile or more out to the fishing grounds. When we reached the spot, Craig had to hang on to the rail with one hand as he cast his line with another.

Almost immediately he had a bite. Not only a bite, he had a big one on the line—it was almost bending his fishing rod in half. Then the fish began to run, and the charter captain and crew began to shout advice to Craig:

"SNUG UP YOUR LINE!" shouted one.

"LET HIM RUN A BIT. BUT DON'T LET HIM BREAK THE LINE!" shouted another.

For the next 20 minutes, as the boat tossed and turned, Craig did his best to follow the shouted instructions, the fish getting closer and closer to the boat.

It was at this point that I noticed Craig's face was turning a light shade of green.

"Are you getting seasick?" I asked.

He just gave me a miserable look and nodded as he continued the battle to land the fish.

The captain and crew continued to call out advice until Craig suddenly handed the fishing rod to them and leaned over the rail, very sick.

Even with experienced fisherman on the line it still took several minutes to bring the near-record-sized walleye on board.

Craig, now pale and shaking, was sitting and staring into space as the captain held the fish by a gill and pushed it in front of his face.

"Look at that," declared the Captain, "it's just a half-inch short of a record."

Craig looked at the glassy-eyed, smelly fish a couple of inches from his nose and turned to hang over the rail again.

He stayed there most of the way into port. When we reached the dock the captain held up the fish again and asked if Craig wanted to clean it on the shore or pack it in ice to take home.

Craig, still a bit green around his own gills, said he didn't even want to look at that fish, or any other fish again as long as he lived.

The fish ended up going home with the captain and crew.

GENEVA STATE PARK

You can often find charter fishing captains at the concession stand at the marina. Marina officials can usually supply you with names and phone numbers of fishing guides.

This is also one of the state parks that offer the rent-a-camp program. If you and your family have never tried tenting or camping before, this is an easy and inexpensive way to try before you invest in all the expensive equipment.

For under $20 a night (rates vary at different parks) you can rent a large tent, complete with gasoline lantern, cookstove, cots, mattresses, ice cooler, picnic table, and fire-ring and firewood. In short, all you have to do is bring blankets and food.

Geneva State Park ☎ (216) 466-8400 marina and park
Padanarum and Lake roads • Geneva, Ohio
Handicapped access: yes

FRESH FRUIT

The area around Geneva and Geneva-on-the-Lake is rich farmland, and you can find many roadside markets offering grapes, apples, and peaches—for which the area is famous. Autumn is the best time to visit for these treats, although many places are open year round. If you like to pick your own apples or grapes, below are a couple of places we have stopped.

You'll also find wineries that offer wine tasting in their stores. One of the newest of the Ashtabula County wineries is the Tarsitano Winery, featuring several wonderful wines. Ken Tarsitano created the winery right on his parent's farm; the barn doubles as a sales room.

Tarsitano Winery ☎ (440) 224-2444
4888 Hatches Corner Rd. · Conneaut, Ohio
Handicapped access: yes

Spring Hill Orchards and Farm Market ☎ (800) 793-4299
6062 S. Ridge West (Rte. 84) · Geneva, Ohio
Handicapped access: yes

Old Firehouse Winery & Restaurant ☎ (440) 466-9300
5499 Lake Rd. · Geneva-on-the-Lake, Ohio
Handicapped access: yes

OHIO'S OLDEST LAKE ERIE RESORT

That's the boast here at Geneva-on-the-Lake, which has been a vacation destination for folks since the mid-19th century. They offer vacation cottages, a mini-amusement park, wineries, and restaurants. For more information contact:

Geneva-on-the-Lake Chamber of Commerce ☎ (440) 466-8600
5536 Lake Rd. · Geneva-on-the-Lake, Ohio

ONE TANK TIP #4

Ask About a Better Room

When registering at a motel, be sure to ask about upgrades to the room you have booked. Some motels and hotels offer same-price upgrades to better rooms if it looks like they will not be busy and the better rooms would be empty.

13 Romance and History

If you're looking for a romantic place to get away to for a weekend or just overnight, Elaine Crane, who operates Rider's Inn in Painesville, has just the answer.

The tavern has been around since the early 1800s providing shelter, food, and beverages for travelers. Today, while still maintaining a historic look, it offers modernized bedrooms with private baths and beautiful furnishings. If you want to surprise someone special, give the inn a call and they can arrange for someone to buy a slinky negligee or robe, in the right color and size, that will be on the bed waiting to be used when you arrive. Also, you can schedule a romantic dinner at the inn and, when you are finished, the hostess will offer to give you a tour of the premises. Upon reaching your room (which is the last stop on the tour), she hands you a key and gently closes the door leaving the two of you alone.

Rider's Inn ☎ (440) 354-8200
792 Mentor Ave. · Painesville, Ohio
Handicapped access: yes

A VERY SPECIAL MAILBOX

When I appear at places like the I-X Center in Cleveland, I usually take along my special One Tank Trip Mail Box. It was made for me by the folks at The Mailbox Factory, in Kirtland. The owner used to drive snowplows and had to repair mailboxes that he knocked over. He did such a good job that neighbors started asking him to build their mailboxes. Today he doesn't plow anymore, he builds mailboxes. Some look like homes, others like cars and trucks, still others resemble animals such as cows and pigs. Whatever your interest, the Mailbox Factory can probably build a mailbox just for you.

The Mailbox Factory, Inc. ☎ (440) 256-MAIL
7857 Chardon Rd. · Kirtland, Ohio
Handicapped access: yes

FARMS AND RAILROADS

Lake Metroparks offers attractions based on farms and railroads and much, much more. For starters, at the Penitentiary Glen Park you can find a miniature steam railroad. A club, whose members build the steam trains, has its headquarters at the park, and, as a condition for using it, when they meet they give free rides on the little trains to kids and adults on a first-come, first-served basis.

Another wonderful attraction is Lake Farmpark. Here you can wander around a barn, help milk a cow, or even take a horse-drawn ride through the park. There are gift shops and restaurants here.

Lake Farmpark ☎ (800) 366-3276
8800 Chardon Rd. • Kirtland, Ohio
Handicapped access: yes

A GARDEN CENTER TOUR

Lake County is one of the garden nursery centers of the country. The many large greenhouse complexes throughout the county make it a wonderful place to tour, especially in the spring. One of the largest growers around is Champion Garden Towne in Perry. You can take a free tour of the place just by giving them a call. They also have a huge garden shop that carries just about anything you need for the garden. Open daily.

Champion Garden Towne ☎ (440) 259-2811
3717 N. Ridge Rd. (U.S. 20) • Perry, Ohio
Handicapped access: yes

ZSA ZSA'S FAVORITE RESTAURANT

You never know when you might run into Zsa Zsa Gabor, of Hollywood fame, here at George's Famous Dinner Bell Restaurant in Painesville Township. George Diskes, the owner, is a friend and confidant of Zsa Zsa's and has hosted her at the restaurant several times.

As for the "Famous" in the restaurant name, that's probably due to the huge portions that they serve here. Their soup has a hump in it, because they pile so much chicken and so many noodles into each bowl. This is also one of the few restaurants I have visited that offers prime rib, with eggs, for breakfast.

George's Famous Dinner Bell Restaurant ☎ (440) 354-3708
1155 Bank St. • Painesville Township, Ohio
Handicapped access: yes

OHIO'S PRESIDENTIAL TRAIL: JAMES A. GARFIELD

The 20th president of the United States made his home in Mentor. Lawnfield is the house Garfield purchased in 1876 and summered in until he was elected president in 1880, when he went to Washington, where he was assassinated just months after taking office.

Lawnfield ☎ (440) 255-8722
James A. Garfield National Historic Site
8095 Mentor Ave. · Mentor, Ohio
Handicapped access: steps in house

Lawnfield

HOLDEN ARBORETUM

Lake County has one of the largest arboretums in the United States. With over 3,400 acres of land, Holden Arboretum contains woods, meadows, and ponds. It is a great place for birdwatchers. You'll find well-marked trails with signs identifying the various trees, wildflowers, and grasses. Especially beautiful in the spring and fall, Holden is a four-seasons desintation.

Holden Arboretum ☎ (440) 946-4400
9500 Sperry Rd. · Kirtland, Ohio
Handicapped access: yes

14 Some People Fly, Some Don't

I was driving with a camera crew on Cleveland's West Side when, crossing a bridge, we spotted what appeared to be a huge kite sailing over the valley near the steel plants. We went to investigate and, on top of a cliff near West 11th Street, we found a group of hang gliding fans practicing their sport.

We watched for a while, did some filming, and were preparing to leave when the leader, Chuck Slusarczyk, asked if I would like to try flying.

Now what they were doing was putting on a harness that was attached to a giant kite-shaped wing, hoisting it over their heads, running, and leaping off the edge of the cliff. Then, lifted by the wind, they would gently float and spiral down to a baseball diamond several hundred feet below in the valley.

Slusarczyk assured me that it was absolutely safe, that all you had to do was point the nose of the kite down to gain speed and point it up to slow or level out. Tip your body—hanging by the harness from the kite—to the right and you would turn right; tip left to turn left. The hardest part, he said, was carrying the kite back up the hill after you landed.

At this point I suffered a total loss of good sense and, egged on by photographers Dave Williams and Ted Pikturna, I somewhat reluctantly strapped on the hang glider. I found myself running pell-mell towards the edge of a cliff, hanging onto a huge kite with white knuckles.

Just as I stepped off the edge into space, I realized this was not the best idea that I had ever had.

The hang glider plummeted about 10 feet, and, as I was closing my eyes to avoid the impact with the earth below, I discovered that I was soaring.

It was like being a bird. I leaned to the right, and the hang glider went into a tight turn to the right. Unfortunately, I was too close to the edge of the cliff to turn, and I went slamming into a debris-littered slope. The impact dragged me over two discarded mattress springs and a patch of broken bottles before I stopped.

As I was counting my arms and legs to see if they were all there, Chuck Slusarczyk came sliding down the hillside.

"You turned too soon," he scolded me, as he helped me to my feet. "You go up there and try it again."

I looked down. My pants were in shreds, and a dozen cuts to my knees and shins were leaking blood into my shoes, and he wanted me to try it again?

"No way!" I said.

"Come on, skin will grow back," Slusarczyk said. "Besides, if you don't go now, you'll be spooked and never try it again. You almost had it. Try it once more."

As I said, I was suffering from a total loss of common sense at the time, because a few minutes later I found myself on top of the hill shakily running again towards the edge of that same cliff.

This time I was expecting the sudden drop, and was determined to just soar straight across the valley to the baseball field. I attempted to slow the speed by raising the front of the hang glider. It was too much and I began to stall! The hang glider peeled off to the right, and I found myself heading right back into the same patch of debris I had landed in on the first attempt.

I was still lying face down on a rusty bed spring when Slusarczyk and some friends reached me. My right pant leg was gone below the knee. I had bits and pieces of broken beer bottles embedded in my knees and shins, but otherwise I was unhurt.

My common sense had finally returned. Despite Slusarczyk's pleas that I try it one more time, I refused.

My photographers, Williams and Pikturna, suggested that I might want to go to a hospital to get the glass out of my legs and to get a tetanus shot.

They dropped me off at the emergency room at St. John Hospital and drove off to cover a fire while I was attended to.

Now, from the waist up I looked O.K. It was from the knees down where I was hurting, and since I was standing in front of her desk, the registrar could not see cuts on my legs.

"What's your problem?" she asked

"I'd like to see a doctor about patching up some cuts."

"How did you get hurt?" she said, not even looking up from the form she was filling out.

"Uh, I don't think you would understand," I replied.

"Try me," she said with some smugness, "I've heard just about everything."

"Okay," I said. "I fell off a kite."

"Sounds to me like you want a psychiatrist, instead of a medical doctor," she said.

You know, maybe she was right.

While I have never flown a hang glider again, I am still fascinated by flight and the men and women who have taken wing.

Each time I drive by the huge dirigible air dock at the old Akron City Airport, I am struck by the sheer size of the historic building. Opened in 1931, the air dock is 211 feet tall, 320 feet wide and 1,175 feet in length, without a single supporting pillar or girder. At the time, it was the largest such building in the world.

They say that you could lay out 10 football fields inside the structure, that the interior is big enough to house two aircraft carriers, the Washington Monument, and the Statue of Liberty. The ceilings are so high that sometimes condensation causes small clouds to form inside the building.

It was constructed by the Goodyear company of Akron to house their giant dirigibles, which nearly filled it completely. For an idea of how big the dirigibles were, today all of their active airships—or blimps—could fit in the space that just one dirigible once took up inside the air dock.

While no public tours are allowed of the inside of the building, it can easily be seen from surrounding roads and highways.

AN AKRON RITUAL

It's not officially spring until Strickland's ice-cream stand opens. The homemade custard, made fresh each day, has been prepared from the same recipe for generations. Strickland's is right across the street from the old Akron Airport, and their parking lot is a good place to see the air dock while enjoying an ice-cream cone. Open seasonally, closed in winter.

Strickland's Frozen Custard ☎
1809 Triplett Boulevard • Akron , Ohio
Handicapped access: limited

STAN HYWET HALL AND GARDENS

The magnificent mansion owned by the Seiberling family, who owned Goodyear, is now open to the public. Its 60-some rooms range from the great hall to a wonderful music room, where Paderewski once played. There is an indoor swimming pool, game room, and formal gardens, which are a favorite with newlyweds for picture backgrounds. During the holidays, the mansion is decorated as it was during the time the Seiberling family lived there.

Stan Hywet Hall and Gardens   ☎ (330) 836-5533
714 N. Portage Path · Akron, Ohio
Handicapped access: yes

Stan Hywet Hall

ROUND HOTEL ROOMS

The only hotel in the world where you can sleep, in luxury, in a silo is at the Hilton Akron at Quaker Square. The old cement silo complex, which once held the oats destined to become Quaker Oats oatmeal, has been made into modern, round hotel rooms. The six-inch-thick concrete walls guarantee privacy and quiet. The hotel also offers several restaurants and a night club. It is also attached to the Quaker Square shopping mall, which offers unique shops and specialty stores. You can even buy an oatmeal cookie fresh from the oven here.

Crown Plaza Quaker Square   ☎ (330) 253-5970
Quaker Square, 135 S. Broadway · Akron, Ohio
Handicapped access: yes

Crown Plaza Quaker Square

WALK UNDER A POND

One of the best metroparks in Ohio is located in Akron. Here, you can walk beneath a mock-up of a farm pond and see pond life from a fish's point of view. This unique building also houses an observation room where, through one-way glass, you can watch wild animals while they feed just outside. The Summit County Metroparks also offer some truly great hiking trails in many of their other parks.

F. A. Seiberling Naturealm ☎ (330) 865-8065
1828 Smith Rd. • Akron, Ohio
Handicapped access: yes

Metroparks Serving Summit County ☎ (330) 867-5511
975 Treatyline Rd. • Akron, Ohio
Handicapped access: yes

AKRON TO CLEVELAND ON A TRAIN

You can actually take a train from Independence to Akron and vice versa. The Cuyahoga Valley Scenic Railroad has begun almost year-round trips from Independence, Ohio, to downtown Akron. When the trains arrive in Akron, buses meet them and carry the passengers to a variety of area attractions. On the way down, there is also a stop at the Western Reserve Historical Society's Hale Farm and Village in Bath, Ohio. You can get off the train and spend an afternoon there, then catch the train to Independence on its return later in the day.

There are plans to one day extend the train from Independence all the way to downtown Cleveland and Canton.

The Cuyahoga Valley Scenic Railroad   ☎ (800) 468-4070
Howard St. at Ridge St. • Akron, Ohio
Handicapped access: steps into cars

Cuyahoga Valley Scenic Railroad

A TOMBSTONE JUST ISN'T A TOMBSTONE ANYMORE

You can take a tour of the North Hill Marble and Granite Company. While most of the business still consists of making tombstones, they also use their talents to serve the living. They offer a really different way to identify your home: a large boulder inscribed with the family name and street number as well as a duck, perhaps, or symbol of a favorite hobby or sport. They also offer small inscribed stones for gardens with poems and quotations.

Getting back to the tombstone business, they also specialize in tombstones for pets. The largest they have ever done was a tombstone for a horse.

North Hill Marble and Granite Company ☎ (330) 253-2179
448 N. Howard St. • Akron, Ohio
Handicapped access: steps in building

SLEIGH RIDES AND CARRIAGE RIDES

When snow is on the ground, you can have a never-to-be-forgotten experience: a sleigh ride in an authentic cutter, pulled by a horse in a harness festooned with bells. It's like a scene from a Currier and Ives print.

The owner, Wade Johnson, builds his own sleighs, which are modern replicas of the famous 19th-century "one horse open sleighs." The rides are taken at his farm, and the paths run over hills and through woods, just like in the song. In fact, he even encourages his passengers to sing.

When the ride is over you are invited back to his carriage barn for hot chocolate or cappuccino and some sweets around the wood-burning stove in his carriage museum.

During warmer weather, when there is no snow, Johnson also has beautiful carriages that provide rides and picnics at nearby Brandywine Falls in the Cuyahoga Valley National Recreation Area. Reservations are always required.

Carriage Trade/Sleigh Rides ☎ (330) 467-9000
8050 Brandywine Rd. • Northfield, Ohio
Handicapped access: limited

A WINTER SPORTS PARADISE

If you like sledding, cross-country skiing, or snowshoeing, you can find all three at the Virginia Kendall Park, operated by the National Park Service. In fact, if you do not own a pair of snowshoes, the park rangers will lend you a pair, free. All you have to do is leave your driver's license. At special times, rangers who are expert on snowshoes will lead visitors on snowshoe walks through the woods and around the lake on winter nature walks. These are also free. Call for times. The sledding hills and cross-country ski trails are open whenever weather permits.

Virginia Kendall Park   ☎ (800) 445-9667
Truxell Rd. • Boston Township, Ohio

PRO BASEBALL UP CLOSE

If you can't seem to get tickets to a Cleveland Indians game, consider an evening or day at their farm club in Akron. The Akron Aeros have their own new state-of-the-art baseball stadium in downtown Akron. While the names of the players may not be familiar, remember that the next Jim Thome, Manny Ramirez, or Sandy Alomar may be playing here right now, just waiting for his big chance.

In any event, the stadium tour gives you a behind-the-scenes look at how a minor league team operates at the beginning of a new century. You'll be impressed by the locker rooms, exercise rooms, and practice rooms housed in the stadium, as well as the public facilities like the restaurant.

The best time to take the tour is on an off-game day, when they take you to the locker room and the dugouts and onto the field. Call the community relations department for prices and reservations.

Akron Aeros   ☎ (330) 253-5153
Canal Park Stadium
300 S. Main St. • Akron, Ohio
Handicapped access: yes

ONE TANK TIP #5

Coupon Clipper Alert

Check the local tourist and convention bureau for free or discount coupons for local attractions, restaurants, and motels.

15 You Never Know About Those TV People

We had set up a booth at the annual outdoor sports and travel show at the giant I-X Center to hand out our One Tank Trips booklets to visitors.

It was about the end of the fifth day that I had been there when a friend, Lieutenant J. P. Allen of the Ohio State Patrol, stopped by. J. P. looks like a recruiting poster for the State Highway Patrol—six-foot-one, sandy-haired, handsome. He was off duty and wearing a flannel shirt and dungarees. I invited him to join me in the booth so we could chat in between visits by viewers.

We had been talking about ten minutes when I got rather busy with several people who had questions. J. P. stood beside me watching the crowd when he noticed an elderly lady studying him.

She would look first at J. P., then study the pictures on the back of the booth. We had posted large color photographs of all our leading anchors: Tim Taylor, Dick Goddard, Casey Coleman, and Tana Carli. Tana, from Alliance, had been a runner-up for the title of Miss America and was the first female evening anchor hired by TV-8.

The lady stood for several minutes looking first at the pictures and then at J. P. Finally she stepped up to the counter.

"Which one are you?" she said, nodding toward the wall of pictures.

"Oh, I'm Tana Carli," he said, jokingly.

"No you're not," the woman declared. "You're a man."

The challenge in the woman's voice was just enough to trigger J. P.'s sense of humor.

"Yes, I am Tana Carli," he replied, moving back to stand beside Tana's picture.

"That's impossible," said the woman again. "You're a man."

"Take a good look and use your imagination," J. P. pleaded, as he held Tana's picture up beside his head. "Picture me with a woman's wig, false eyelashes and some makeup, and wearing a dress."

J. P. smiled at the lady with his best Tana Carli smile.

She stared at J. P. and the picture, her face showing confusion.

"But you're a good-looking man, why would you want to dress up like a woman?" the lady finally blurted.

"Well, it's this way. I wanted to get into television, but they didn't have any openings for men at the time, and so I decided to apply as a woman," he answered, with a straight face.

The lady still wasn't totally buying his story.

"If you're Tana Carli, let's hear you say something like she says it," she challenged.

Without batting an eye, J. P. raised Tana's picture in front of his face and said, in a falsetto voice, "The attack of the killer parakeets; next on Newscenter 8."

Now, J. P. does not sound a bit like Tana Carli, but the power of suggestion must have been at work as he held the picture in front of his face because the woman's mouth dropped open.

"MY GOD! You really are her!" she exclaimed.

From behind the picture J. P. gave me a wink.

"I just can't believe this is really true," the woman continued.

I was struck by a fit of coughing and excused myself from the counter.

J. P. was just warming up.

"Did you like that sweater I was wearing on the news show last night?" he asked the woman.

"Uh, yes," the lady replied. "It was quite attractive."

"I bought that at Value City," he said. "I just love bargains, don't you?"

The more they talked, the more convinced the lady became that J. P. was indeed Tana Carli.

Finally an elderly man, obviously the woman's husband, wandered up to the booth.

"You ready to go yet?" he asked her.

"You're never going to believe who this man is," the woman gushed at her husband.

Before he could guess, she blurted out: "This is Tana Carli, on TV-8!"

"Go on!" Her husband responded.

"No, really," she said. "He wears a wig and a dress when he's on television."

"Woman, have you lost your mind!" he retorted.

The woman turned to a smiling J. P.

"Put the picture in front of your face and talk to him like Tana," she pleaded.

So J. P. complied, and, again, the power of suggestion apparently overcame reason as the man stepped back, studied J. P., and said, "I'll be damned!"

As the couple wandered off, still shaking their heads we could hear the man telling the wife, "You just never know about those TV people."

INDOOR FERRIS WHEEL

The huge, sprawling I-X Center was built on the edge of Cleveland Hopkins International Airport during World War II. At times it has served as a bomber and tank plant, turning out weapons of war for both World War II and Korea.

In recent years it has been turned into the largest exhibition hall in the country. Here is an illustration of just how big it is. Once, when the Republicans were considering the I-X Center for their national convention, it was pointed out that the president could pull Air Force One right inside it.

I-X Center Indoor Amusement Park

In fact, there are 20 acres under one roof here, and one of the more unique ways this space is used is as an indoor amusement park each spring. The 10-story-high Ferris wheel stays year round and is used even when other shows are running at the center. Popping through the roof is the largest indoor Ferris wheel in the world. The amusement park is seasonal, late March–early May.

I-X Indoor Amusement Park   ☎ (216) 676-6000
6200 Riverside Dr. • Cleveland, Ohio
Handicapped access: yes

ASTRONAUT ICE CREAM

At the other end of Cleveland Hopkins International Airport you will find the NASA Lewis Research Center. The visitor center offers an interesting look into the work being done here, as well as exhibits tracing the history of airplanes and space flight. There is also a nice gift shop in the visitor center where you can buy space souvenirs, including Astronaut Ice Cream. It's dried ice cream that has a plastic appearance, yet when you place it in your mouth it tastes just like the real thing.

Visitor Center, John Glenn Research Center, NASA   ☎ (216) 433-2001
21000 Brookpark Rd. • Cleveland, Ohio
Handicapped access: Handicapped Access: yes

THE CLEVELAND METROPARKS

Also bordering Cleveland Hopkins International Airport is part of the Cleveland Metroparks system. The Rocky River Reservation offers picnicking, fishing, bridle trails and stables, golf, baseball diamonds, sledding hills, all-purpose trails, a marina, and a great place to just relax on a nice day. It's all part of the "Emerald Necklace" chain of metroparks surrounding Cleveland.

Cleveland Metroparks   ☎ (216) 351-6300
4101 Fulton Parkway • Cleveland, Ohio
Handicapped access: yes

16 A Real Human Fly

"Our company sold several of them to Buckingham Palace in England," the man on the telephone declared.

"A personal fire escape system?" I replied.

"That's right," the salesman responded. "If your bedroom is above the first floor you ought to have one of these."

When the man offered to come to Cleveland to give a demonstration by climbing down the front of a downtown building, I agreed to do a story on his product.

A week later Charles Morgan arrived at our studios. He had some bad news; his arm was in a sling. Due to a sprained wrist, he would be unable to demonstrate the personal fire escape for me. But not to worry, he said, "This system is so easy to use that one of the princes at the Palace uses it to sneak out of his room. Why don't you try it?"

"I get nosebleeds when I stand on a chair," I pointed out.

"All you have to do is sit in this sling," he said, "and hang onto this rope. Just feed it out at the speed you want to be lowered to the ground."

He was holding up a series of rather sturdy-looking ropes and a wide canvas belt. The idea, he said, was to go up on the roof of our four-story building and find a suitable place to tie the ropes, then place the canvas sling around my rear end and just step over the edge and lower myself to the ground.

Shortly, I found myself standing on the roof of the TV studio. The ropes had been tied to an iron pipe, snaked over the sandstone ledge, and draped down the building side to Euclid Avenue.

My first concern came when I noticed Morgan looking at an instruction book that came with the fire escape. A puzzled look now and then flitted across his face.

"Are you sure this is really safe?" I asked, as I looked over the edge of the roof and felt butterflies grow in my stomach when I realized how far down four stories could really be.

"Oh, absolutely!" he replied. "Our ropes are one hundred percent guaranteed. If one should ever break, for any reason, we replace it, without charge to you."

I was just about to ask what good a new rope was going to do me if I fell four stories when I noticed a demonstration down on the street. Videographer Ralph Tarsitano, who had been assigned to film my descent, had organized a group of bystanders, who were chanting, "Jump! Jump! JUMP!"

Tarsitano saw me peering over the edge of the roof.

"Hey! Would you mind either climbing down here, or jumping. It's just about time to go to lunch!"

Back on the roof, Morgan was nervously strapping me into the harness. I noticed his hands were shaking. Just then our general manager, Chuck Bergeson, strode onto the scene.

"You don't have to do this!" he said sternly. "Just remember, you don't have to do this, and if you get hurt there won't be any worker's compensation."

With that, he whirled and stomped off.

With all of this support I felt I just had to try it. I carefully pulled the rope taut and sat down on the edge of the roof. The chanting— "Jump! Jump!"—was still going on, with Tarsitano now leading it.

I closed my eyes and pushed off. I swung out, then slammed back into the brick building. I wasn't going anywhere. I was just hanging there!

"You've got to let go of the rope so it will pay out the line!" shouted Morgan from above me, still holding the instruction book.

I timidly let go of the rope and immediately dropped almost six feet before I again snatched the rope in a death grip and my descent was checked.

I now found myself hanging between the top of the building and the windows on the third floor. I opened one eye and could see fellow workers behind the windows waving at me. I weakly smiled at them and then looked down. It was a big mistake. The bottom of the Grand Canyon would have appeared closer than the street, three stories below me.

A brisk wind was now whistling down Euclid Avenue, and I began to swing on my perch, blown back and forth by the breeze. The word "terrified" would not adequately describe my feelings at that moment.

"PAY OUT THE ROPE!" Morgan was shouting from the roof, still clutching the instruction book.

Inch by inch I let the rope slide through my hands, suddenly realizing that I could control the rate of my descent down the building. I had just reached the level of the top of the first floor windows when Morgan leaned over and shouted something that I could not understand.

He was still shouting something as my trembling legs touched the sidewalk and I half-collapsed against the side of the building. I was greeted by a smattering of applause from bystanders. I was still standing there when Morgan burst through the front door, still clutching the instruction book. His face was white as a sheet.

"Are you all right?" he gasped

"Yeah, I'm fine," I replied. "What were you trying to tell me as I got near the bottom?"

"That the rope was breaking!" he responded.

It turned out Morgan had never actually used the harness himself, and it was the first time he had ever had someone demonstrate it. When we strung the ropes over the edge of the sandstone at the top, he forgot to put a rubber pad between the rope and the stone. The result was that every time I swung back and forth on the rope it grated across the sandstone lip, cutting the rope. Only a few strands of nylon still held it together as I reached the sidewalk. Next time, I think I'll just take the elevator.

THE TERMINAL TOWER

While it no longer holds the title of Cleveland's tallest building (Key Tower now has that honor), I still get a thrill from the view atop this landmark. If you have never enjoyed the 360-degree view of Cleveland that pigeons see every day, you have missed a real experience. For more than 60 years the sight of this office tower has spelled "Welcome" to visitors from all over the world and especially to Clevelanders returning home. The 42nd-floor observation deck is open on weekends only.

Terminal Tower Observation Deck   ☎ (216) 621-7981
50 Public Square · Cleveland, Ohio
Handicapped access: yes

A BIG CORNED BEEF SANDWICH

Rave all you want about your Chicago corned beef sandwiches. I say Cleveland is the Corned Beef Capital of America. Just drive through the downtown area and count the number of diners and small eating places that specialize in the briny brisket.

A tiny restaurant on St. Clair is where I usually go to satisfy my cravings for the salty red meat. Here, they carve it thin and pile it high on fresh rye bread—almost four inches high. Then they slather it with mustard and pile on a heaping tablespoon of some potent horseradish. My eyes water at the memory of this lunchtime treat.

Danny's Deli   ☎ (216) 696-1761
1658 St. Clair Ave. • Cleveland, Ohio
Handicapped access: step into restaurant, narrow crowded aisles

THE U.S.S. *COD*

Not many Great Lakes states have a submarine parked on their waterfront. The U.S.S. *Cod* was a fighting ship in World War II. After her wartime service, she was brought to Cleveland to be used by the Navy Reserve for training. When she was declared surplus and it looked like the submarine would be scrapped, a citizens' group was formed and funds were raised to have her made into a floating museum with a permanent home on Cleveland's lakefront.

U.S.S. *Cod*

The sub has been kept in original World War II condition. That means to get in and out you have to squeeze through hatches and climb up and down ladders just like the crew did more than 50 years ago. It's not an ideal place for skirts and high-heeled shoes.

U.S.S. *Cod*   ☎ (216) 566-8770
1089 E. 9th St. • Cleveland, Ohio
Handicapped access: Ramp to deck. Narrow hatches and ladders into submarine

EDGEWATER STATE PARK

The 100-acre park that sits on Cleveland's front step is one of my favorite spots to take visitors for a view of the Cleveland skyline. From an outlook called Perkins Beach on the western end of the park (accessible from the shoreway), you can see one of most impressive views of Cleveland, with tall buildings spiking into the sky. In the foreground, rolling waves hit the shore of Edgewater State Park. The park offers swimming, boating, exercise trails, fishing, and even kite-flying areas. It's one of the city's favorite playgrounds.

Edgewater State Park ☎
6700 Memorial Shoreway · Cleveland, Ohio
Handicapped access: yes

LAKE VIEW CEMETERY

Out-of-town friends are usually taken aback when I suggest we visit a cemetery. But Lake View Cemetery isn't your average burial ground. It started out as an arboretum and still has an impressive display of trees and flowers in the springtime. It is also the final resting spot of President James A. Garfield, tycoon John D. Rockefeller, inventor Charles Brush, and many other notables of Cleveland's—and the nation's—past. Cemetery officials actually encourage visitors to walk, hike, even picnic in the cemetery.

Lake View Cemetery ☎ (216) 421-2665
12316 Euclid Ave. · Cleveland, Ohio
Handicapped access: yes

THE CUYAHOGA COUNTY ARCHIVES

This interesting old building is the repository of all of the county records. Here you can find a description of Elliot Ness's apartment when he lived on Lake Avenue and a copy of George Burns and Gracie Allen's marriage license (they were married here while appearing at Play House Square). There are gruesome pictures of Kingsbury Run murder victims from the coroner's old files. If you are looking into your family's history, they have records dating back to the founding of the city—back when a bounty was paid by the county commissioners for killing wolves. It's a fun place to spend a rainy day.

Cuyahoga County Archives   ☎ (216) 443-7250
2905 Franklin Ave. • Cleveland, Ohio
Handicapped access: steps into building, narrow aisles

ALADDIN'S BAKERY

Have you ever wondered how pita bread is made with a pocket? Well, wonder no more. Just take a tour of Aladdin's Bakery. You can watch as the pitas come from the oven, looking like small basketballs, to be pressed flat by packers. Aladdin's is also a great place to sample some Middle Eastern foods like falafel, tabbouleh, and, of course, pita bread.

Aladdin's Bakery   ☎ (216) 861-0317
1301 Carnegie Ave. • Cleveland, Ohio
Handicapped access: yes

LOLLY THE TROLLEY

Even if you have lived in Cleveland all of your life and know every side of the city, I think you will be surprised at what you learn on one of Lolly the Trolley's tours of Cleveland. The driver/guides are not only very personable, but also very knowledgeable and will give you some new insights into the town. It's fun for strangers and residents alike. You can find Lolly at Burke Lakefront Airport and the Powerhouse in the Flats. For reservations call:

Lolly the Trolley   ☎ (216) 771-4484
Call for tour information • Cleveland, Ohio
Handicapped access: steps into trolley

ANOTHER HALL OF FAME ON THE LAKEFRONT

Burke lakefront Airport is now the official home of the International Women's Air and Space Museum. The museum, which operated for several years in Centerville, Ohio, honors women's contributions to space and air travel. Exhibits feature such women as Amelia Earhart (one of her flying suits will be on display) and Sally Ride, the first American woman in space.

International Women's Air and Space Museum   ☎ (216) 623-1111
1501 N. Marginal Rd. • Cleveland, Ohio
Handicapped access: yes

NORTHWEST OHIO

17 Ohio's Presidential Trail: Rutherford B. Hayes

After the state of Virginia, Ohio has the highest number of native sons who became president of the United States. They came from just about every corner of the Buckeye State, starting with a transplanted Virginian, William Henry Harrison, in North Bend, Ohio, near the Ohio–Indiana border, and ending with Warren G. Harding of Marion. In between there was Civil War hero Ulysses S. Grant, born in Point Pleasant, at the bottom of the state, and James Garfield of Mentor. There was also William Howard Taft of Cincinnati, and William McKinley of Niles and Canton. Benjamin Harrison was the grandson of William Henry Harrison and was born at his grandfather's farm in North Bend. The president who is possibly the least known, but who left perhaps the biggest legacy to the state of Ohio, is Rutherford B. Hayes.

Hayes, known as "Ruddy" to his friends, had a distinguished record as congressman, governor of Ohio, and Civil War general. He was elected to the presidency in a disputed election that saw the outcome decided by an electoral commission. Hayes pledged not to run for reelection. In his inaugural address he summed up his feelings with these words: "He serves his party best, who serves his country best."

Hayes was credited with helping bind up the wounds of the Civil War by ending the rule of carpetbaggers in the South. He also rooted out corruption in government and helped establish the civil service.

When he was done with his one term, he came back to Ohio, to Spiegel Grove, his home in Fremont. Here he lived out the rest of his life. His son, Medal of Honor winner Col. Webb Hayes, encouraged the state to build a library dedicated to his father's memory on the estate grounds he donated; it was the first presidential library in American history.

Today the Hayes Presidential Center in Fremont honors not only President Hayes but also all the men who have served as the nation's chief executive. In the museum there are exhibits honoring each of the presidents.

The beautiful Victorian mansion where Hayes lived is also kept almost as it was in his day and is open to the public.

President and Mrs. Hayes were buried on the estate. His grave is covered with a simple stone that has only his name. There is no mention that he once was a general, governor, and president of the United States.

Rutherford B. Hayes Presidential Center   ☎ (800) 998-7737
Spiegel Grove • Fremont, Ohio
Handicapped access: limited

Hayes Home

SHOPPING AT THE PRESIDENTIAL CENTER

Don't overlook the bargains to be had at the Hayes Presidential Center. Rare books from the library are often on sale, as well as limited-edition Christmas ornaments and several one-of-a-kind items for history buffs. No admission charge to enter museum store.

Hayes Presidential Center Museum Store   ☎ (800) 998-7737
Spiegel Grove • Fremont, Ohio
Handicapped access: partial access

OTHER THINGS TO DO IN FREMONT

Scuba diving in a quarry is one of the things you can do in the Sandusky County Park System in and around Fremont. At White Star Park there is a bathing beach and an abandoned quarry that is filled by clear springwater, which, according to divers, makes this one of the better places in northern Ohio for practicing dives.

Wolf Creek Park offers camping along a winding river not far from Fremont.

Sandusky County Park District   ☎ (419) 334-4495
1970 Countryside Dr. · Fremont, Ohio
Handicapped access: yes

From My Mailbag...

Dear Mr. Zurcher,

Please send me everyThing you know. I have enclosed a self-addressed sTamped envelope.

P.S Please leT me know if you need more Than one sTamp.

18 Sandusky Bay

I had the opportunity a couple of years back to see Sandusky Bay from a point of view usually reserved for birds.

Some friends suggested that I try parasailing. That's riding a parachute attached to a boat that tows the chute with you hanging from beneath it—the chute, not the boat.

I had seen all these videotapes of poor, misguided middle-aged men and women who had been talked into a similar ride. You see them running as fast as they can on a beach as a speedboat heads for deep water. A long rope tied to the person on the shore gets taut and then slams them, face first, into the sand and drags them through the water.

"That's not for me," I told my friend.

"We don't do it that way," he insisted. "It's just like sitting in a rocking chair, only one that flies 300 feet in the air over the lake."

So, on a sunny morning I found myself with videographer Bob Begany in the back of a strange-looking speedboat on Sandusky Bay. The rear of the boat was covered with a large square platform. I was told to put on a life jacket and a harness and to sit on the platform.

The boat sped up and a crew member unfurled a huge parachute off the rear of the boat. Tow straps attached to two stanchions held the parachute down.

Once it was filled with air, the crew member motioned for me to step up to the stanchions and told me to grab the straps. As I did, he transferred the snaps from the stanchions to my harness.

Before I had time to ask what to do next, I felt myself suddenly lifted into the air by the parachute. An electric winch began to pay out line, letting me go higher and higher as the boat picked up speed.

I soon found myself floating hundreds of feet over Lake Erie, the boat now looking like some small water bug dashing across the lake below me.

It was very pleasant up there. I could even see the distant Canadian shoreline. I was still clinging to the straps above my head with a white-knuckle grip, but I was beginning to relax and almost enjoy the trip when I noticed that I was starting to sink towards the water.

The boat was heading into the wind and was unable to keep up enough speed to keep me in the air, and I was slowly floating closer and closer to the surface of Lake Erie.

I was ready to take a deep breath before hitting the water when I stopped going down and seemed to just hover over the surface of the water. My feet occasionally touched a wave, as the boat gained enough speed to keep me floating just over the surface.

The boat turned and started running away from the wind, and I soared back into the sky. This time I noticed, as we rose higher and higher away from the roar of the boat's motor, that all I could hear was the creak of the nylon harness stretching and making strange noises as it adjusted to the pull of the rope and to my weight. I began to get a mental image of what it would be like if the harness suddenly broke and I dropped 200 feet to the water below. It made me grab the straps all the more tightly over my head!

A few minutes later I felt myself being lowered again, but this time I was being reeled in by the rope and I was headed towards the boat, not the water. In seconds I gently stepped down onto the surface of the boat, and the crew member quickly tied the chute onto the stanchions, releasing me.

I was more than a little proud of myself for having taken such a daring ride, and looked to the young crew member expecting him to congratulate me on being so cool on my roller coaster–style ride, when he turned and said: "You were a bit nervous up there. Last week I had an 85-year-old lady up celebrating her birthday. You should have seen her," he said with admiration. "She insisted on taking her camera with her. She shot three rolls of film and changed film in the camera twice while she was up there."

North Coast Parasail   ☎ (419) 627-2279
On the beach at Cedar Point • Sandusky, Ohio
Handicapped access: sandy beach to boat

CRUISE TO THE ISLANDS

A wonderful way to see Sandusky Bay and the Lake Erie Islands is to take one of the many cruise boats that offer day-long cruises through the bay and around the islands, stopping at several before heading back to Sandusky that evening.

Mailing address: 1006 East Strub Road, Sandusky, Ohio 44870.

Goodtime I Cruises   ☎ (419)625-9692
Jackson St. Pier • Sandusky, Ohio
Handicapped access: yes

A MERRY-GO-ROUND MUSEUM

This is one of Sandusky's most unusual attractions. The old post office building, with its rotunda, has been turned into a carousel museum featuring an actual working merry-go-round and exhibits of carousel horses and figures from around the world. There are also demonstrations by a carver who makes and repairs the figures. A gift shop is also on the premises. Tours are available, and you can also ride the merry-go-round. Open year round.

Musum of Carousel Art & History   ☎ (419) 626-6111
Corner West Washington & Jackson streets • Sandusky, Ohio
Handicapped access: yes

HISTORIC JOHNSON ISLAND

During the Civil War, Confederate officers were imprisoned on an island in Sandusky Bay. Some escaped, while others died or were killed here. Today, a Confederate cemetery and a statue of a Confederate soldier are all that remain of this tragic chapter in Sandusky Bay's history. The cemetery is open to visitors (there is a toll gate fee) and can be reached by boat or by causeway from the mainland. The rest of the island is strictly private.

Confederate Cemetery ☎ (no telephone)
Johnson Island · Sandusky Bay, Ohio

Courtesy Cleveland Press Collection (CSU)

Johnson's Island Confederate Cemetery

FISH DINNERS

The local folks have a couple of favorite places where they enjoy fresh Lake Erie perch dinners. The decor at each is basic "neighborhood hangout," but the folks are friendly and the food is good.

DeMore's Fish Den ☎ (419) 626-8861
302 W. Perkins Ave. · Sandusky, Ohio
Handicapped access: ramp to door, restrooms not handicapped accessible

A BIG ICE-CREAM CONE

Toft's Dairy of Sandusky is an institution. Generations of Sanduskians have made a pilgrimage to this dairy store on a summer's day for a single, double, or triple ice-cream cone. Newcomers get a real surprise. Their "single" is really two large dips of ice cream; there are three dips for a "double"; and a triple—well, you have to have a milk-shake cup to keep all the dips upright on the ice-cream cone. It's a true ice-cream lover's kind of place.

Toft's Dairy and Ice Cream ☎ (800) 521-4606
3717 Venice Rd. (Rte. 6) • Sandusky, Ohio
Handicapped access: yes

East Side Café ☎ (419) 627-1964
1319 First St. • Sandusky, Ohio
Handicapped access: steps into building

FLYING OVER THE BAY

Griffing Flying Service has been providing a lifeline year round to the folks on the Lake Erie islands for 65 years.

The airline offers both island flights and sightseeing flights over the entire Sandusky Bay area.

Griffing Flying Service ☎ (419) 626-5161
3115 Cleveland Rd. • Sandusky, Ohio
Handicapped access: yes

BEST MILK SHAKE

One of the best milk shakes I've had in recent years can be found in a most unusual place: the snack bar here at Griffing Flying Service's Sandusky Airport. They make it with several dips of ice cream, and they test it by standing a straw up straight. If the straw leans, they put in more ice cream.

Snack Bar, Griffing Flying Service ☎ (419) 626-5161
3115 Cleveland Rd. • Sandusky, Ohio
Handicapped access: yes

ONE TANK TIP #6

Good Timing Pays Off

When possible try to travel in the off-season winter and early spring months, for bargain prices and a better choice of hotels and motels.

19 The Island

Whop! Whop! Whop!
Whop! Whop! Whop!
Through my closed eyelids I could see the shadow of the propeller as it flashed over my head. It was like the opening scene of *Apocalypse Now*, except this was not a movie—this was real, and I was lying on my back on a small island while a real helicopter hovered just a few feet above me.

What had brought me to Starve Island, a tiny spit of sand jutting out of Lake Erie off South Bass Island, was an idea that videographer Bill West and I had cooked up to illustrate the joys of an island One Tank Trip. Starve Island is about 30 feet long and 6 feet wide. We pictured a final shot that would show me sleeping in the sun and then, as the helicopter lifted higher and higher, would reveal me on a private island in the middle of Lake Erie.

Helicopter pilot Andy Overley had outfitted his craft with pontoons for this shoot, and we waited until late afternoon when the sun would be in just the right position. It looked like everything was going to work perfectly. We circled the tiny island a couple of times before starting down. We noticed several seagulls take off, but gave them little thought. Andy was more concerned with the number of rocks sticking up at uneven angles. He finally decided that it would not be possible to set down on the island, but that he could hover just a foot or so off the rocks. I could sit in the doorway and just step out, and when I got in position, he would then lift straight up.

The downdraft from the helicopter blades set up a veritable whirlwind of feathers and sand as we sat hovering over the rocks. I shielded my eyes from the wind and quickly stepped out and lay down on the greenish rocks with a child's innertube beneath my head for a pillow. I heard the "Whop! Whop! Whop!" of the blades as Andy applied more power to lift off. I peeked out of one eye and could see the lens on Bill West's video camera two feet away from my face and starting to lift away.

As the helicopter soared into the sky and the wind from the propellers lessened, I became aware of some new sensations. The rock was wet and slippery. It also smelled. Just then I heard it: the sound of angry seagulls! Opening both eyes I saw the sky above me filled with seagulls. I was lying in the middle of a smelly seagull rookery, and around me were several nests! I scrambled to my feet and frantically waved at the helicopter, which was now wandering 2,000 feet in the air along the edge of South Bass Island. We had agreed that when they took off Andy and Bill would then shoot the outline of the bigger islands before coming back to retrieve me.

For the next 15 minutes I used the small plastic innertube and my hat to scare off angry gulls that kept zooming in closer and closer, scolding me with their raspy voices. I also realized that my back, from head to toe, was covered in slimy bird dung. It was just about the longest 15 minutes of my life!

Finally, the helicopter came back, and I clawed my way back inside, much to the amusement of pilot Overley and videographer West—amusement that lasted until the smell of my guano-soaked clothes intensified in the heat of the helicopter's bubble cockpit. We then made a high-speed run to the nearest landing strip in Port Clinton.

Bird droppings aside, the Lake Erie islands make a wonderful place for a getaway for the weekend, a week, or all summer—and winter, too.

Perry Victory and International Peace Memorial

SOUTH BASS ISLAND

The Perry Peace Monument on South Bass Island, 352 feet high, dominates the skyline. From the observation platform at its top, on a clear day, you can see the Canadian shoreline. Park rangers will point out where Commodore Oliver Hazard Perry defeated the British Fleet during the War of 1812. The monument also serves as a grave marker for British seamen whose bodies washed ashore after the battle.

Besides all the history, the memorial is also a great spot for viewing all the islands.

Perry Victory and International Peace Memorial　☎ (419) 285-2184
Bayview Ave. • Put-in-Bay, Ohio
Handicapped access: grounds and restrooms, yes; memorial, no

PERRY'S CAVE

Legend has it that Commodore Perry stored ammunition in this 52-foot-deep cave on the island. A natural limestone cavern, it is open during summer months for tours.

Perry's Cave and Gemstone Mining　☎ (419) 285-2405
Catawba St. • Put-in-Bay, Ohio
Handicapped access: yes for gemstone mining and gift shop; no for cave tour

WINERY AND CAVE

Heineman Winery, right across the street from the Perry Cave, has its own cave as a tourist attraction. The difference is that Crystal Cave has the world's largest celestite crystals. It is unlike any cave you have ever been in. Upstairs, in the winery and garden, you can sample some of the famous island wines.

Heineman Winery and Vineyards　☎ (419) 285-2811
Crystal Cave
Catawba St. • Put-in-Bay, Ohio
Handicapped access: limited

WINTERTIME ON THE ISLAND

There is a second tourist season here: wintertime. That's when ice fishing attracts hundreds to the vastness of a frozen Lake Erie. Many of the island's summertime fishing guides also are experts on ice fishing and provide little heated shacks and transportation onto the ice to catch some trophy walleyes. A guide we have used in summer and winter is:

Pat Chrysler, Fishing Guide   ☎ (419)285-4631
Put-in-Bay, Ohio

FLY INN BED-AND-BREAKFAST

This new building offers perhaps some of the most luxurious and modern rooms on the island. Some of the bedrooms have private baths and one even has a whirlpool tub. They also offer a swimming pool for the kids and—get this—the place is located right on the airfield. That means the airplane that brings you to the island can pull right off the runway to the front door! The owner is also a pilot with his own plane and offers a package weekend that includes a sight-seeing flight around the islands.

Fly Inn Bed-and-Breakfast   ☎ (419) 746-2525
Dwelle Lane • Kelleys Island, Ohio
Handicapped access: yes

GETTING TO THE ISLAND

In the summertime you can either fly or float to the island. But when winter comes, the airplane becomes the islanders' only link with the mainland for travel, emergencies, and food as there is air service to the islands year-round.

Griffing Flying Service   ☎ (419) 626-5161
3115 Cleveland Rd. • Sandusky, Ohio
Handicapped access: yes

Newman Ferry Service   ☎ (800) 876-1907
101 E. Shoreline Dr. • Sandusky, Ohio
Handicapped access: yes

ONE TANK TIP #7

Midweek Travel Can Be Easier

When possible try to travel midweek. You will usually find a better selection of rooms available as well as shorter lines at popular attractions than on weekends.

20 The Mystique of the Woollybear

You can usually tell if a person lives in northern Ohio by whether they know that a woollybear is a caterpillar and not a four-legged bear with a heavy coat.

My colleague at WJW-TV, Dick Goddard, the dean of Ohio weather forecasters, has raised the lowly woollybear caterpillar to near-legendary status. I mean, how many worms do you know that have a festival named after them?

It all started in my living room back in the 1970s. The local elementary school Parent Teachers Association officers were holding a meeting there one evening as I arrived home from work.

"Does anyone have any idea how we can raise some money?" one of the ladies asked.

"Start a festival named after that woollybear caterpillar that Goddard is always talking about," I said, as I passed through the room.

"If we did," another woman said, "would he make a personal appearance at the festival?"

"Probably," I yelled back from the kitchen. "If you start the festival, I'll ask him."

They did, and Dick did. He not only made a personal appearance; he has been spearheading the festival for more than a quarter of a century. It is now the largest single-day festival in Ohio, attracting upwards of 150,000 people to watch a two-hour parade through the streets of Vermilion, where the festival is now held. There are also races, games, and woollybear look-alike contests for kids and pets. My personal favorite is the woollybear races. This is where anyone who has a woollybear caterpillar can enter him in a race. It's so exciting. Almost as much fun as watching, say, paint dry, or grass grow.

In all seriousness, the festival has remained true to Dick's original concept. All of the proceeds go to charity. None of the TV or radio personalities, including Dick, make any money from the festival, which has raised thousands of dollars down through the years for local organizations and provided northern Ohio families with a wonderful way to spend an autumn afternoon. The festival is held each year at the end of September or beginning of October, depending on the Cleveland Browns schedule. (Dick is the statistician for the team and so has to schedule the festival when the Browns aren't playing.)

The Woollybear Festival   ☎ (440) 967-4477
Vermilion Chamber of Commerce
Liberty St. • Vermilion, Ohio
Handicapped access: yes

The "Woollybear 500" race at the Woollybear Festival

PIZZA AND OTHER PIES

If you have a pie lover in your home, then be sure to make a stop at this pie shop in downtown Vermilion. They make pizza pies here that are very good. But their fruit pies are what brings the tourists back time after time. They make deep-dish pies here that are man-sized. Some of the berry pies weigh two pounds or more.

Mama Jo's Pizza and Pies   ☎ (440) 967-7330
5590 Liberty St. • Vermilion, Ohio
Handicapped access: yes

GREAT LAKES LORE

One of the attractions in Vermilion year round is the Great Lakes Historical Society Museum. Here you can find parts of Commodore Oliver Hazard Perry's flagship, which was sunk in the War of 1812.

There is an actual lake freighter wheelhouse, where you can stand and see the lake through the windows. The museum also has an extensive display of artifacts from famous ships that sailed Lake Erie and the other Great Lakes as well.

Inland Seas Maritime Museum   ☎ (440) 967-3467
Great Lakes Historical Society
480 Main St. • Vermilion, Ohio
Handicapped access: yes, but some steps in museum

A CAPTAIN'S GUEST HOUSE

One of the newest places to spend the night in Vermilion is a Victorian guest house just one block from the lake and two blocks from historic Harbourtown. It has three guest rooms, all with private baths and all air-conditioned. For breakfast, they offer fresh fruit and a sour cream coffee cake that closely resembles the coffee cake that came from the famous Vermilion bakery, Schwensen's, which, sadly, closed in 1994 after being a Vermilion institution for more than a century.

The guest house offers a large wraparound porch that is a favorite of guests during the summer. The house is located within walking distance of many attractions.

Captain Gilchrist Guest House/Bed-and-Breakfast   ☎ (440) 967-1237
5662 Huron St. • Vermilion, Ohio
Handicapped access: steps to second floor and bedrooms

SOME HOMEMADE CHOCOLATES

There is a new candymaker in town. Bob Brummer is the third generation of his family to make chocolates. His family's candy is well known in New Jersey. Bob married a lady from Vermilion and decided to bring his expertise to Ohio. They offer dozens of flavors of chocolates, all made fresh in the candy kitchen at their store. They will even custom pack a gift box of your favorite chocolates, if you give them some advance notice. They also offer more than 18 varieties of sugar-free candy.

Brummer's Homemade Chocolates   ☎ (440) 967-2329
672 Main St. • Vermilion, Ohio
Handicapped access: yes

21 **Camp Perry**

One of my memories of growing up during World War II is riding my bicycle to the front gate at Linwood Park, in Vermilion, where we spent our summers, and sitting on an embankment along the edge of U.S. Route 6. I would come there early in the morning to watch a military parade go by. A convoy of Army trucks, led by jeeps with mounted machine guns, passed by Monday through Friday, taking German prisoners from the prisoner-of-war stockade at Camp Perry in Port Clinton to their jobs in quarries and farms in northern Ohio.

Many of the prisoners were captured during the Normandy invasion. They wore U.S. Army fatigues with a large "PW" painted on each pant leg and across the backs of their shirts. They were mostly very young—men in their teens and twenties, blond-haired and blue-eyed, who appeared to be happy about their situation as prisoners. They would smile and wave to me as they passed. Once in a while one of prisoners would throw me a pack of chewing gum when the jeeps, filled with military policemen, were not too close.

Being only nine years old at the time, I only knew that these men were enemies and I was supposed to hate them. I returned their waves by thumbing my nose at them. However, it was hard to dislike someone who threw gifts and who seemed glad to see you. When they had passed by, I scrambled to the edge of the road to collect the packs of gum they had thrown to me. I never told anyone where I got the hard-to-find treat.

It was many years later, when I was serving with the U.S. Marine Corps Reserves and we were spending a weekend at Camp Perry to practice our marksmanship, that I made a connection with those German prisoners of my youth.

We were staying in small tar-papered barracks at the base and, one evening while I lay on my cot, my eyes strayed to some rafters above me. There, scratched in pencil, were German words, a swastika, and some dates from 1944. These had been the barracks those German prisoners had lived in. Actually, thousands of Germans, and, earlier, Italians, had been held captive here. In fact, the last two thousand German prisoners were still at Camp Perry in

1946, nearly a year after the war ended, before they were repatriated to Germany.

Today the camp still serves as the home of the National Rifle Matches, the premier shooting event in America, held late each summer at the base.

Camp Perry is now home to the Ohio National Guard and was used in recent years as a training base for reserve forces called up for the Gulf War.

The base is open to the public. There is a small museum at the auditorium commemorating the National Guard unit from Port Clinton that was captured by the Japanese on Bataan in World War II. The post also boasts the largest fishing pier on Lake Erie, which also is open to the public. There is a motel available on the post. Reservations are required.

Camp Perry   ☎ (614) 336-6214
S.R. 2 • Port Clinton, Ohio
Handicapped access: yes

CHARTER FISHING

Some of the best charter-boat fishing on Lake Erie can be found in the Port Clinton area. The downtown dock has a host of charter boats available. The favorite catches here are walleye and Lake Erie perch. There are also "headboats"—boats where you can walk on board with your fishing gear and, for a nominal sum, spend the morning or afternoon fishing with many others in one of the lake's best fishing spots. A charter service we used was:

Shore-Nuf Charters   ☎ (419) 734-9999
Drawbridge Marina
247 Lakeshore Dr. • Port Clinton, Ohio
Handicapped access: steps into boat

ELECTRIC TRAINS

In nearby Marblehead, there is a summertime exhibit of electric trains that will warm the heart of any model railroader. A huge room is filled with hundreds of trains in just about every gauge from the tiny N-gauge to the large German style (G-gauge). The exhibit is open daily, all year.

Train-O-Rama   ☎ (419) 734-5856
6732 E. Harbor Rd. (Rte. 163 E.) • Marblehead, Ohio
Handicapped access: yes

SMOKED RIBS

This restaurant has offered hickory-smoked ribs, ham, and turkey as its trademark for years, and is also well known for its signature salads. The only drawback is that it closes during the winter months.

The Crow's Nest Restaurant   ☎ (419) 734-1742
2170 N. Buck Rd. • Marblehead, Ohio
Handicapped access: yes

A FAST WAY TO THE ISLANDS

A 3,500-horsepower hydrojet catamaran is the fastest ferryboat working Lake Erie. The craft can carry nearly 400 people at a time and makes the run from downtown Port Clinton to Put-in-Bay on South Bass Island in just about 20 minutes. It's a refreshing way to get there, but a word of caution: there are no public bathrooms on board the ship.

The First Island Co-Jet Express   ☎ (800) 245-1538
5 Jefferson St. • Port Clinton, Ohio
Handicapped access: yes

22 A Historic Privy

In the town of Genoa is one of the most unusual structures ever placed on the National Register of Historic Places: a privy.

Back during the 1976 bicentennial, the local townsfolk wanted to contribute something to the national birthday. They had thought about their town hall, which was nearly 100 years old, but just couldn't stir much excitement about the project because the building was in such bad shape, and it would cost nearly a million dollars to restore its Victorian architecture.

The town faced a crisis. What to do? Then someone suggested the old privy behind the high school. Built in 1865, it was even older than the town hall. The privy was still standing and wouldn't cost much to restore. It was a sturdy brick building that contained no fewer than 12 seats, divided between two rooms with four doors: one for men, one for women, one for boy students, and one for girl students. The privy had fallen on bad times since indoor plumbing became all the rage.

The historic privy of Genoa, Ohio

Mrs. Aldo Bergman, of Genoa, led the fight to preserve the privy. She and other volunteers raised all the money and labor needed to restore the building in time for the nation's bicentennial celebration. She admits that all those involved in the project took a lot of ribbing, first from townspeople and then from the national media, when word of their quest for historic recognition for the privy got out. But the federal government took it seriously and granted the little privy national historic status. In fact, Mrs. Bergman says, Congressman Delbert Latta accepted an invitation to be the principal speaker at the dedication ceremony for the outhouse.

And that wasn't the end of the story. Federal officials were so impressed with the efforts of the "save the privy" group that they gave the community a $750 million grant to fix up their town hall and list *it* on the National Register of Historic Places, too—which is exactly what the volunteers had wanted to do in the first place.

There is probably a moral to this story, but I am not exactly sure just what it is. However, if you should happen to be in Genoa, be sure to stop and take a look at possibly the only privy in the nation listed, officially, as historic.

A BATHROOM MUSEUM

Also in Northwest Ohio, and related in theme, is perhaps the only museum in Ohio that spells out the history of the bathroom. At Archbold, Ohio, you will find the Sauder Craft Village and Farm. This is a collection of historic buildings from the Northwest Ohio area. At the rear of the village, in a large building, is an eclectic museum that is chock full of all kinds of equipment and paraphernalia used on early farms. In one corner is an exhibit that traces the history of the bathroom, complete with toilets of every description, bathtubs, and sinks.

The village contains many living history exhibits featuring volunteers, dressed in the costumes of a century ago, still demonstrating crafts such as broom making, blacksmithing, yarn spinning, and herb gardening. There are real farm animals, buggy rides, and barns to wander through. Nearby is a restaurant where fresh country foods are served each day.

If you would like to stay here, check out the newest attraction: the Sauder Heritage Inn, opened in 1994. It is a beautiful, rustic, barn-like inn with large, attractive rooms, each with a private bath. Breakfast is included in the price of a night's lodging.

Sauder Heritage Inn   ☎ (800) 590-9755
Historic Sauder Village
S.R. 2 • Archbold, Ohio
Handicapped access: yes to both inn and village

SOME BARGAINS ON FURNITURE

Erie Sauder, who founded the Sauder Craft Farm and Village, made his fortune from inexpensive furniture. Many years ago he founded Sauder Furniture, which today is sold across the country in KMart, Wal-Mart, and many department stores. The furniture is office and home items such as desks, entertainment centers, bookcases, and beds, much of it made from particle board and sold unassembled. The main plant is in Archbold. A factory outlet here sells discontinued models, overruns, and some factory seconds—pieces that may have cosmetic blemishes but be perfect in every other way. You often can find these types of items at a savings here.

Sauder Outlet Store   ☎ (419) 446-2711
Lugbill Rd. and S.R. 66 · Archbold, Ohio
Handicapped access: yes

A MOST UNUSUAL CAR DEALERSHIP

The sign outside reads "Used Cars for Sale," but this place is more museum than showroom. To be sure, some of the collectible Cadillacs and Peerless automobiles on display are for sale; these are mostly duplicates of other collectible cars this dealer owns. The huge garage has dozens of autos from the early part of this century, all the way up to some of the most modern Cadillacs. The showroom-museum also contains an eclectic collection of signs, bottles, musical instruments, old washing machines, advertising, and many other collectible items. There is an admission charge. They are usually closed on weekends and open only Monday through Friday.

Oberhaus Enterprises, Inc., Cars and Collectibles   ☎ (419) 446-2773
1488 S. Defiance St. (S.R. 66, South) · Archbold, Ohio
Handicapped access: yes

LADDERS AND NAKED FURNITURE

Another factory store in this town offers a strange variety of things, from ladders to "naked" furniture (that's furniture with no stain or finish). Like at most factory stores, the best deal here is usually on items being discontinued, or on production overruns.

Archbold Furniture Company Outlet Store   ☎ (419) 446-3235
303 E. Mechanic St. · Archbold, Ohio
Handicapped access: no

23 The Wandering Statue

Just outside Toledo, in the town of Perrysburg, stands a statue that spent many years trying to find a home. Most people who drive by this monument to Commodore Oliver Hazard Perry, hero of the Battle of Lake Erie, don't realize how much it has traveled.

Back in 1860, veterans of the War of 1812 honored Perry with a statue in the center of Cleveland's Public Square. It stayed there a while, but, wouldn't you know, along came progress: the city fathers decided to cut the square into quadrangles. After much debate, Perry's statue was moved to the new southeast quadrant, where it was expected to remain forever. Wrong. In the 1890s, veterans of the Civil War wanting to commemorate their service cast their eyes on Commodore Perry's corner of Public Square. By then most of the vets of the War of 1812 were gone, and the veterans of the latest war got their way. The Perry Monument was carefully taken down to make room for the new Soldiers and Sailors Monument.

But what to do with Commodore Perry? A home was eventually found in Gordon Park, overlooking Lake Erie. But the monument was showing years of wear, and it was decided that a new statue of the good commodore should be cast for placement there. Now the question was, what about the old statue?

A group of patriotic citizens in the small town of Perrysburg had followed the debate over the commodore's statue and now contacted Cleveland officials. Since their town was actually named after the commodore, why not give them the old statue? Although there is some debate over whether the statue was actually given to the town or whether they had to pay for it, the old monument indeed ended up there, where it still stands today.

Nearby is Fort Meigs, which, like the statue, dates back to the War of 1812. The largest reconstructed fort in America, it covers several acres overlooking the Maumee River. The fort was built to defend against the British in the War of 1812 and was abandoned after the war. Today, in summer, staff members at the fort wear the uniforms of the 1812 period and demonstrate weapons used at the fort.

Fort Meigs State Memorial ☎ (419) 874-4121
State Rte. 65 • Perrysburg, Ohio
Handicapped access: gravel paths

THE TOLEDO FIREFIGHTER MUSEUM

A former fire station in the city of Toledo has been put to an excellent use. It has become a museum where much of the Toledo department's old equipment is now on display and real, active-duty firefighters are assigned to teach fire safety and to recall a proud history to visitors.

Tour guides point out such things as an early lantern from the days when firemen still pulled their pumper to the fire by hand. The youngest member of the department would take the lantern and run ahead of the sweating firemen hauling their pumper down the street screaming at the top of his voice, "FIREMEN COMING! FIREMEN COMING!" He was sort of the predecessor of the siren and red light used today to clear the way for fire trucks. The museum also offers a look at how firemen lived a hundred years ago. There are shiny brass poles down which they would slide when answering a fire alarm. Call for hours of operation. Admission is free.

Toledo Firefighter Museum   ☎ (419) 478-3473
918 Sylvania Ave. • Toledo, Ohio
Handicapped access: yes

A FACTORY STORE

This umbrella factory has been a downtown Toledo landmark for over half a century. You're invited into the building where they assemble all kinds of umbrellas. While you can't stroll through the factory aisles, you can see what's happening from the company's store, where they sell some of their discontinued models at a considerable savings. You can also order anything in their catalog.

Haas-Jordan Company   ☎ (419) 243-2189
1447 Summit St. • Toledo, Ohio
Handicapped access: steps into plant

OHIO'S ONLY ERIE-FRONT LODGE

Of all the state parks in Ohio, only one offers a lodge with a view of Lake Erie. Maumee Bay State Park is also the newest addition to Ohio's chain of state-operated parks. The property is located just east of Toledo and includes not only a modern lodge with indoor and outdoor swimming pools and an exercise room but also tennis courts and a state-of-the-art golf course. Futuristic-looking, furnished cabins are also available, scattered along the edge of the golf course on the north side of the park. The park is located only minutes from downtown Toledo and is also very close to the Port Clinton-Sandusky Bay area.

Maumee Bay State Park Lodge

☎ (800) 282-7275 Ohio State Park reservations; (419) 836-1466 local
1750 Maumee Bay Park Rd. #2 • Oregon, Ohio
Handicapped access: yes

CORPORAL KLINGER'S FAVORITE RESTAURANT

Jamie Farr, who portrayed the character Corporal Klinger on the popular TV show *M*A*S*H*, really did grow up in Toledo, Ohio. The Tony Packo's Restaurant that he used to recall with fondness on the TV show really does exist. In fact, Tony Packo's is a Toledo institution. The walls are covered with—believe it or not—autographed hot dog buns, some of them bearing the names of customers like former president Jimmy Carter and Burt Reynolds! As for the food, spicy Hungarian hot dogs and chili sundaes are a couple of the specialties. The tavern is a very popular spot for lunch and dinner, so be prepared to wait for a seat.

Tony Packo's Café   ☎ (419) 691-6054

1902 Front St. • Toledo, Ohio
Handicapped access: restrooms not accessible

A TOUR TRAIN

The Toledo area has one of the oldest-running tourist trains in Ohio: the Bluebird has been operating between Waterville and Grand Rapids, Ohio, for nearly 20 years. The trip covers a 10-mile stretch along the Maumee River and ends with the dramatic crossing of a long bridge over the river. The operating times change with the seasons. Call for hours.

Bluebird Passenger Train   ☎ (419) 878-2177

The Toledo, Lake Erie and Western Railroad
49 N. Sixth St. • Waterville, Ohio
Handicapped access: steps into train

A GLASS OUTLET STORE

Toledo is the world headquarters of the Libbey Glass Company, and local folks know that a good spot for bargain glassware is the Libbey Factory Outlet at the factory. You can buy their discontinued stock, as well as seconds (cosmetically flawed glassware that can't be sold in stores) at a good savings.

Libbey Factory Outlet   ☎ (419) 254-5000
205 E. Erie St. • Toledo, Ohio
Handicapped access: steps into store, narrow aisles

A MUSEUM SHIP

A 600-foot-long lake freighter has become a permanent part of the downtown skyline in Toledo. The ship, which once hauled ore and steel through the Great Lakes, has been retired and turned into a floating museum. Be aware that a lot of walking and climbing are required to see this exhibit.

S.S. Willis B. Boyer Museum Ship   ☎ (419) 936-3070
International Park • Toledo, Ohio
Handicapped access: no

A MEXICAN-GERMAN KIND OF PLACE

The operators of two Toledo restaurants, one of German ancestry and the other of Hispanic heritage, decided to merge their eateries into one establishment. The result: a delightful mix of ethnic cultures and food. Where else can you get a platter of sauerkraut and tacos? Seriously, the combination seems to work. The kitchen turns out specialties of each culture; customers can order straight German, straight Mexican, or mix them as they desire. The restaurant has become very popular; reservations are a must, especially on weekends.

Fritz and Alfredo's Restaurant   ☎ (419) 729-9775
Mexican and German Cuisine
3025 N. Summit St. • Toledo, Ohio
Handicapped access: ramp to restaurant, restrooms not accessible

A MUSEUM WHERE YOU CAN TAKE HOME THE PAINTINGS

Wouldn't it be nice ... you go to an art museum, see a painting you like—and buy it to take home and enjoy every day. Sounds like fiction you say? Not really. The famous Toledo, Ohio, Museum of Art has been doing just that since the 1970s.

Now, I don't mean that if you see a Rodin or a Van Gogh in the museum you can just take it off the wall and head to the cash register. It doesn't quite work that way. While they have some of the world's most famous art on display, that isn't for sale. But they do have this great department in the museum called Collector's Corner, where they offer artwork work for sale—perhaps not by old masters, but for the most part by artists who are recognized professionals. Paintings, glass, textiles, and works in other media are on display, and for sale. For a few dollars—or several thousand dollars— you can take home one of their juried works of art.

At one time many museums offered area artists a chance to show and sell their works. Today, the Toledo Museum of Art is exceptional for its strong commitment to helping aspiring artists not only display but sell their work. Admission is free.

Toledo Museum of Art   ☎ (419) 255-8000
2445 Monroe St. • Toledo, Ohio
Handicapped access: yes

Toledo Museum of Art

CENTRAL OHIO

24 Memory Food

Does the mention of a fried bologna sandwich stir memories? Do you find yourself back in kindergarten? Well, there is a restaurant in central Ohio that has made fried bologna sandwiches an art form. The G & R Tavern in the small town of Waldo, south of Marion, offers a unique sandwich. It is made of a half-inch-thick slab of homemade bologna that is grilled to a crusty dark brown, covered with a slice of Monterey Jack cheese, topped with large slices of sweet onion and sweet pickle, then flipped onto a fresh Kaiser roll. To some, it is possibly the closest thing to true ambrosia.

It started back about 32 years ago when the original owners, two men named George and Roy, decided to put a fried bologna sandwich on the menu. It wasn't anything unusual. Waldo is farm country, and many a young farmer carried fried bologna sandwiches to school each day, especially in the 1930s, '40s, and '50s. Well, George and Roy's new dish must have touched off memories, because their fried bologna sandwich became an instant hit. Their fame spread far from the only downtown street in Waldo. The news reached Columbus, and local newspaper food writers drove up Route 23 to see what all the fuss was about. Soon, food mavens from around the state were stopping in for a fried bologna sandwich. Television personalities from all over also started to get a nostalgic craving for the kindergarten soul food. More publicity followed.

Today a sign on the side of the building proclaims, "Best fried bologna sandwich in America." If you challenge that statement, the staff of the G&R will probably whip out a guest book that has comments from across the country by many who claim to have driven long distances just to taste their fried bologna sandwich. They can tell you that each week the little country tavern goes through over a half-ton of the specially made bologna. The ingredients are a closely guarded secret that will only be revealed to whoever buys the tavern. If it is ever sold.

If you visit the G & R, chances are you might find a nun sitting on a barstool next to a truck driver, with both enjoying a fried bologna sandwich. Also, it is not unusual to see people carrying large grocery bags filled with the sandwiches when they leave.

G & R Tavern   ☎ (740) 726-9685
103 N. Marion Rd. (U.S. 23) • Waldo, Ohio
Handicapped access: step into building

A POPCORN MUSEUM

How many towns can claim a museum dedicated to popcorn? Marion, Ohio, can. The Wyandot Popcorn Company is located here, and their collection of popcorn machines and popcorn wagons has finally found a permanent home at the city's new Heritage Hall. The museum also includes a huge stuffed horse, exhibits reflecting other industries that once called Marion home, and a room dedicated to the memory of the town's most famous son, former U.S. president Warren G. Harding.

Wyandot Popcorn Museum / Heritage Hall   ☎ (740) 387-4255
169 E. Church St. • Marion, Ohio
Handicapped access: yes

Wyandot Popcorn Museum

PRESIDENT WARREN G. HARDING

Although some might say there is a definite correlation between bologna and politics, I choose to think it is just coincidence that a few miles north of Waldo is Marion, the home and burial place of the last U.S. president to come from Ohio: Warren G. Harding.

The Harding home is just as he and Mrs. Harding left it in 1920 to go to Washington. President Harding died in office and was brought back to Marion to be buried in a magnificent tomb just a mile or so from his home.

Though Harding's administration was racked with scandal and many of his appointees went to prison, Harding himself was never charged with wrongdoing. Some historians paint him as a man who relied too much on the advice of political cronies, while others are quick to point out that the good things he accomplished in office have been largely forgotten. One bit of interesting Harding trivia is the following phrase from a speech he gave in 1923: "We must have a citizenship less concerned about what the government can do for it, and more anxious about what it can do for the nation." Some believe it was that half-forgotten speech that inspired President John F. Kennedy's more famous line 40 years later.

Home and small museum open for tours; admission charged.

President Harding Home   ☎ (740) 387-9630
380 Mount Vernon Ave. • Marion, Ohio
Handicapped access: steps into house and inside house

25 Touring with the Governor

I have had many memorable trips over the years, but one that particularly sticks in my mind was a dinner by candlelight in a century-old log cabin tucked away in the hills of southern Ohio. Our hosts were the governor and first lady of Ohio.

It all started when Governor George Voinovich invited my wife, Bonnie, and me to join him, with his wife, Janet, and a group of travel writers from around the United States on a bus tour of some tourist attractions in southern Ohio. The trip was aimed at boosting Ohio tourism by exposing writers to what the Buckeye State has to offer, and showing how important tourism is to Ohio by having the state's chief executive lead the tour.

One of the out-of-state writers later told me that she had accepted the invitation just to see if the governor would really show up to take part in the tour. She said she expected him to just drop in sometime over the weekend, give a speech to the writers, and then depart, leaving his underlings to lead the tour. The writer joined the tour just as the bus was leaving. When we arrived at our first destination, she asked when the governor was going to arrive and was shocked to learn that the nice couple she had been chatting with on the bus—the ones wearing sweatshirts and walking shoes, who had just introduced themselves as George and Janet—were the governor and first lady.

In fact, the governor and Mrs. Voinovich didn't exactly lead the tour. They just joined the rest of us in wandering in and out of attractions, asking as many questions as the writers did of the people in charge at each destination.

The first evening ended at the Inn at Cedar Falls, a hundred-plus-year-old log cabin and complex located in the heart of the Hocking Hills State Park. It was a beautiful Ohio autumn night, and candles glowed in each of the cabin's windows. Inside, innkeeper Ellen Grinsfelder and her staff had been working to prepare a gourmet feast for the writers and the governor and his staff. During dinner, the governor and Mrs. Voinovich table-hopped, talking with all of the writers and reminiscing about their affection for the Hocking Hills area. The governor said he had first discovered it when he was a student at nearby Ohio University. Janet Voinovich remembered the times when their children were small and the whole Voinovich family would rent a cabin for a vacation in the area.

Our accommodations for the night were in a converted barn located behind the cabin. Each of the rooms, while rustic, had a bathroom and electricity—but no TV, no radio, and no clock! As the dinner ended, we wandered up to our rooms, the path illuminated only by moonlight.

In the morning we were fed a wonderful gourmet breakfast and had time to wander the gardens around the cabin where many of the herbs and vegetables for the dining room are grown.

The inn sits in the middle of the 10,000-acre Hocking Hills State Park. It is only minutes away from some of Ohio's most famous attractions, like Old Man's Cave and Ash Cave, with miles of trails to hike and wonderful rock formations to see. While autumn is spectacular here, each season lends a special beauty to the park system.

Inn at Cedar Falls   ☎ (800) 653-2557
21190 S.R. 374 · Logan, Ohio
Handicapped access: yes

Hocking Hills State Parks
☎ (740) 385-6165 camping; (740) 385-6841 park office
20160 S.R. 664 South · Logan, Ohio
Handicapped access: yes

A STEAM TRAIN RIDE

One of Ohio's first steam excursion trains is located in nearby Nelsonville. The railroad, operated by volunteers, uses both steam- and diesel-powered engines to give tourists a slow ride through the Hocking Valley. Tickets can be obtained at the depot in Nelsonville. The train usually runs seasonally, but does make special runs on holidays. Call for schedule.

Hocking Valley Scenic Railway
☎ (614) 470-1300 Mon–Fri; (740) 753-9531 Sat–Sun
US 33 at Hocking Pkwy. · Nelsonville, Ohio
Handicapped access: no

BARGAIN BOOTS

You can buy some boots at bargain prices and take a tour of the boot factory in Nelsonville. This is where the famous Rocky boots are made. The factory outlet store sells seconds and overruns at a considerable savings. Tours are available when the plant is in operation. The outlet store is open Monday through Saturday.

Brooks Shoe Company   ☎ (740) 753-3130
Canal St. • Nelsonville, Ohio
Handicapped access: steps in plant

COLLEGE FOR HOTEL MANAGERS

There is a most unusual motel in this town. The Hocking Technical College operates the facility as a training ground for its students in hotel management, restaurant management, and several other related fields. The motel is staffed by advanced students and supervised by instructors. Often the service and food are superb, but you have to keep in mind that this is a training facility. It is an inexpensive place to stay and eat while visiting the area.

Ramada Inn, Hocking   ☎ (800) 221-2222 reservations; (740) 753-3531
S.R. 691 • Nelsonville, Ohio
Handicapped access: yes

From My Mailbag...

Neil Zurcher

My friends and I took your advice and went to an Amish restaurant. We were looking forward to what you described as "real Amish food." We were very disappointed when the waitress brought us fried chicken, roast beef, and mashed potatoes and gravy. We can have this at home. We were expecting real ethnic food. What a disappointment.!!

--Unhappy in Euclid

26 The Forgotten Governor

John Brown of Medina served as lieutenant governor of Ohio longer, and under more governors, than any other lieutenant governor in the state's history. He wanted to be governor of Ohio and unsuccessfully ran for the office at least once. He was never elected to the top office, but through an unusual chain of events he finally succeeded in becoming the state's chief executive—if only for 11 days.

Back in 1957, when Governor Frank Lausche succeeded in his attempt to win a U.S. Senate seat, he resigned as governor 11 days before his term ended. Lausche wanted to be sworn in early in Washington to gain a few days' seniority over other freshman senators. Under Ohio's laws of succession, John Brown became the governor for those last 11 days of Lausche's term.

Now, no one expected Brown to do much more than just be a caretaker and sort of keep the governor's office running until fellow Republican C. William O'Neil, who had been elected to succeed Lausche as governor, took office 11 days later.

Brown decided if he was going to be governor in name, he would also be governor in fact. He and his wife immediately moved into the governor's mansion on East Broad Street. They held a reception and invited any Ohioan who wanted to see where the chief executive lived.

He addressed the state legislature, pleading for additional school funding and calling their attention to the problems resulting from the rising urbanization of rural areas. He also called for conservation of Ohio's natural resources.

In his 11 days in office, he also called the two sides together in a troublesome telephone strike in southern Ohio and was instrumental in hammering out a settlement.

Perhaps the most controversial thing he did as governor was to commute the first-degree murder convictions of four prison inmates to second-degree murder, making them eligible for parole.

When his 11 days were over, he quietly moved out of the governor's mansion and returned to his hometown of Medina. In later years he would be elected again and again to the office of lieutenant governor, but never to the top job. Nevertheless, during 11 days in 1957, John W. Brown of Medina truly was the governor of Ohio.

THE STATE CAPITOL

On 10 acres in the center of Columbus, at the intersection of Broad and High streets, the business of Ohio is conducted. The statehouse, some critics say, looks like a wheel of cheese on a box. Others point to the Greek Doric structure with pride and claim it is unique among America's state capitol buildings. It contains the state house of representatives, senate, supreme court, and the offices of various top state leaders, including the governor.

The rotunda is open for tours seven days a week. Tours of legislative chambers and offices in the building can be arranged Monday through Friday.

The Ohio Statehouse ☎ (614) 466-2125
Broad & High St. • Columbus, Ohio
Handicapped access: yes

COSI

It stands for Center Of Science and Industry. It is really a hands-on, fun place for the entire family.

There is always something new at COSI, from the kids' room on the second floor—where they can have water fights and not get wet—to the steel beam in front of the building, where anyone brave enough to do it can ride a bicycle 20 feet off the ground in relative safety to prove a scientific theory of balance.

COSI ☎ (614) 228-2674
333 W. Broad St. • Columbus, Ohio
Handicapped access: yes

COSI

SLATE RUN FARM

I have long said that Ohio's greatest treasures are the metropark districts that abound in the state. These local parks get very little statewide publicity and many are almost unknown, yet they offer everything from caves, canyons, and scenic vistas to wonderful state-of-the-art nature exhibits and a host of other things to do for the entire family.

In Columbus, the Metropolitan Park District operates the Slate Run Farm, located in nearby Pickaway County. The farm is frozen in time. It is just like it was at the turn of the 20th century. Horses are still used to till the earth. The farmhouse still uses wood cookstoves. The workers here are all in period costumes and stay in character when responding to questions. Kids are allowed to help with chores, like gathering eggs and cultivating the garden by hand, or use an old rope swing under a tree beside the farmhouse.

Slate Run Farm   ☎ (614) 891-0700
Metropolitan Park District of Columbus
9139 Marcy Rd. • Ashville, Ohio
Handicapped access: steps into some buildings; farmhouse not accessible

A REALLY BIG BURGER

German Village in downtown Columbus is an example of what can be done with a deteriorating neighborhood. Private capital, over the years, has restored much of this ethnic community from a slum to an attractive residential neighborhood and popular dining area. One of my favorite spots is an old tavern that serves one of the largest hamburgers in Columbus. Called a "Thurmanburger," it contains nearly one pound of ground meat, cheese, ham, and condiments. It's more than a meal, all by itself.

Thurman Cafe   ☎ (614) 443-1570
183 Thurman Ave. • Columbus, Ohio
Handicapped access: narrow aisles, crowded dining area

CATALOG BARGAINS

Have you have ever wondered what happens to that merchandise you sent back to J.C. Penney's catalog service center? It ends up in a giant outlet store in Columbus.

The store is located right next to the catalog distribution center, and returned merchandise, along with discontinued items, is offered for sale. The merchandise is constantly changing, so there is always something new. A careful shopper can save up to 50 percent on some items.

J. C. Penney Outlet Store   ☎ (614) 868-0250
2361 Park Crescent Rd. · Columbus, Ohio
Handicapped access: yes

A MOTORCYLE MUSEUM

One of the more unusual museums in the state is located in the Columbus suburb of Pickerington. It features the history of motorcycles, from the earliest models, which were made on wooden frames, to the most modern types from all over the world.

Motorcyle Hall of Fame Museum   ☎ (614) 856-2222
33 Collegeview · Pickerington, Ohio
Handicapped access: yes

GOURMET PEANUT-BUTTER-AND-JELLY SANDWICHES

The Krema Nut Company knows a lot about peanut butter. In fact, they are the oldest peanut butter company in America. They were formed way back in 1898 and have been churning out chunky and smooth peanut butter ever since.

This past year Krema opened perhaps the only sandwich shop in Ohio—and the country—dedicated to the peanut-butter-and-jelly sandwich. The shop offers a dozen "gourmet" PB&J combinations that really melt in your mouth. Manager Brian Giunta loads up homemade wheat or white bread with hearty sloshes of Krema's chunky or smooth peanut butter (all natural—no additives), and then spreads delicious preserves, like strawberry jam or orange marmalade, on top. If you can dream it and it contains PB&J, Brian will try to make it for you.

Krema Nut Company   ☎ (614) 224-9252
400 N. High St. · Columbus, Ohio
Handicapped access: yes

A HAMBURGER MUSEUM

The original Wendy's Old Fashioned Hamburger Restaurant is still standing and, in fact, is still serving Wendy's hamburgers. Now it has also been turned into the official Wendy's Museum. Featuring memorabilia like the original homemade dress worn by Wendy Thomas (for whom the hamburger chain is named) and even the first skillet that founder Dave Thomas used to sample hamburger that he was buying for his restaurant. For laughs, they have a video machine that shows some of the outtakes of Dave Thomas's Wendy's commercials. Admission to the museum is free. You can see it while you are eating lunch—at Wendy's, of course.

For information, write to: Wendy's International, 4288 West Dublin-Granville Road, Dublin, Ohio 43017, (614) 764-3327.

Wendy's Museum ☎
Wendy's Old Fashioned Hamburgers
257 E. Broad St. • Columbus, Ohio
Handicapped access: yes

THE LAST WHISTLE

A Columbus firm holds the distinction of being the last American manufacturer of whistles—the kind policemen, referees, and band directors use. They also make the 24-karat-gold-plated presentation whistles that are given each year to the officials in the Superbowl game. They call this model "the most expensive whistle made." It sells for about $60. By the way, these presentation whistles are available to the public. They make a nice gift for a friend or relative that uses a whistle.

The factory is open for tours during working hours, but reservations are required.

American Whistle Corporation ☎ (800) 876-2918
6540 Huntley Rd. • Columbus, Ohio 43229, Ohio
Handicapped access: yes

27 'Tis the Season

After all the holiday stories I have done down through the years, I still believe that one of the best places to give yourself a holiday boost is in the restored canal town of Roscoe Village in Coshocton.

They begin the season with an outdoor candle-lighting ceremony about the first weekend in December. A special guest is usually asked to be the "official candle lighter." I had been invited and arrived on a very cold and dark December night. The town looked like a page from some Dickens novel, with frost painting the edges of windows. Guides from the various attractions in the village were all dressed in 19th-century frock coats or hoop skirts. Streetlights from another era illuminated the walks and roadways, where thousands of people milled about waiting for the ceremony to begin.

A stage had been placed halfway down the main street, White-woman Street. On one side of the street was a steep hillside that led upwards to the next street. On the other side were the stores that had serviced canal boats and their crews a hundred years before.

A brass ensemble was wandering the streets playing Christmas carols, while small groups of carolers strolled in front of the stores singing the songs of the season.

My duties were simple. I was given a brief introduction, to polite applause, and as I stepped forward to the podium, the lights along the streets went out. I struck a match and lit a candle I was holding. For a moment, as I wished the crowd a Merry Christmas, I held in my hand the only light on the street. In the darkness several thousand people stood crowded around the stage.

I walked across the stage and, leaning forward, started to light candles held by the crowd. The light spread outward from my candle and, in moments, pinpoints of light had climbed the hill behind me and ignited a river of candles in the street around me. I led the crowd in the song "Silent Night." Never before had the song seemed so real, so personal, as it did this magical night in Roscoe Village as I stood bathed in the light of thousands of candles.

The restored canal town of Roscoe Village is open year round to tourists. Many of the shops and stores have been re-created as living history museums, where you can watch long-ago crafts still being practiced by experts. There are also antique stores, and a host of places to eat and buy souvenirs and the crafts created in the village. For more information contact:

Roscoe Village Foundation   ☎ (800) 877-1830
381 Hill St. • Coshocton, Ohio 43812, Ohio
Handicapped access: yes

RIDE A REAL CANAL BOAT

The *Monticello III* is a concrete replica of the boats that once traversed Ohio canals. Today, instead of hauling freight, it carries tourists on hourly runs over a mile-long stretch of the old canal. The boat is pulled by a pair of workhorses and follows the same towpath that was used over a century ago. The canal boat ride is only available during the summer months.

***Monticello III* Canal Boat Ride**   ☎ (740) 622-7528
Lake Park • Coshocton, Ohio
Handicapped access: steps into boat

FOLK MUSIC INSTRUMENTS

Early musical instruments used by pioneers and canal workers can still be purchased here, including hammer dulcimers (or mountain dulcimers), banjos, and guitars. This small music store near the edge of the canal offers quality instruments and music.

Wildwood Music   ☎ (740) 622-4224
672 White Woman St., Historic Roscoe Village • Coshocton, Ohio
Handicapped access: steps into building

WHERE TO STAY

One of the nicest places to stay in the village is the Roscoe Village Inn. Built to blend in with its historic surroundings, it appears to be centuries old yet contains all the modern amenities, like private baths, televisions, and restaurants. There are also several bed-and-breakfast establishments in the village.

Roscoe Village Inn   ☎ (800) 237-7397
200 N. Whitewoman St. • Coshocton, Ohio
Handicapped access: yes

AN OLD-FASHIONED HARDWARE STORE

Here in Roscoe Village you'll find a hardware store that will sell you just one nail, bolt, or nut. It's been a hardware store for over a century, and many of the things they sell haven't changed much since the store served the canal boats that once traveled through here. Part museum, with displays of old miniature steam engines, and part store, with straw hats and nail-pullers for sale, it's like stepping into the past.

Roscoe Village Hardware   ☎ (740) 622-0504
Roscoe Village
Whitewoman St. · Coshocton, Ohio
Handicapped access: step into store, narrow aisles

From My Mailbag...

Dear Neel Zurker,

Why do you drive a Tank??? Why can'T you drive a car like everybody else??

--Perplexed

28 The Fastest-Growing Tourist Area in Ohio

The largest Amish population in the world is not in Lancaster, Pennsylvania; it is in Ohio, in Wayne, Holmes, and Tuscarawas counties. These plain people, who reject cars for horses and buggies, and electric lights for kerosene lamps, draw millions of tourists to Ohio each year.

Traditional cottage industries are now being joined by new tourist-oriented businesses that are springing up like Amish flower gardens throughout the region. New inns and bed-and-breakfasts are being added almost daily. Restaurants that feature the Amish "meat and potatoes" cuisine also are appearing at nearly every crossroads. Cheese factories that once relied almost totally on supermarket sales around the state are enlarging their facilities and opening new showrooms, selling their product to tourists so fast that it hardly has time to age. Tour buses wander quiet back roads, leaving plumes of dust behind them as they search out quilt shops and home bakeries. Portions of State Route 39 have been enlarged to four lanes to handle the increased traffic that sometimes creates big-city traffic jams in crossroads villages in the region.

If you are going to be visiting this busy tourist area, here are some things to remember to make your trip more pleasurable.

Don't visit on a Sunday. You will find almost everything closed. The Amish are very religious and do not believe in working on the Sabbath. Many non-Amish merchants, who respect the Amish beliefs, also are closed. If you do plan a Sunday trip, be sure to call ahead to the attractions you want to visit to be sure they are open.

Try to slate your trip for the middle of the week. Weekends are very busy and roads are crowded, as are shops, stores, and restaurants. Even during weekdays, plan on standing in line at many of the more popular restaurants. The very best time to visit Amish country is in the off-season, November through April, on a rainy day, in the middle of the week. You often have the stores and attractions to yourself. Also it's a time when there are price savings at many of the inns and bed-and-breakfast establishments.

When dealing with the Amish, leave your camera in the car. The

Amish do not like to have their pictures taken; it violates their religious beliefs. If you must take a picture, ask permission first, don't just stick the camera in their faces and fire away.

Take a cooler or ice chest with you, especially in hot weather, to take advantage of the many good fresh foods that are for sale in Amish country, like cheese, homemade pies, bread, fresh bacon, and hams. If you forget your cooler, try to schedule your trip so that the place where you are picking up the food items is the last stop before you start home.

Wear comfortable clothes and be prepared for your car to get very dirty. Many of the roads are gravel and dirt, and there is always dust and mud to contend with. Also, be especially careful and courteous on the roadways. Many blind hills suddenly reveal a slow-moving Amish buggy on the other side. And be patient when trapped behind a buggy. Remember that the horse might be frightened by a blast from your automobile horn.

If you plan to spend the night and like to end your day with an alcoholic beverage, be sure to bring it with you, because most of the Amish area is "dry." There are few bars in the small villages, and most of the inns and bed-and-breakfasts do not offer alcoholic beverages. There are exceptions in Millersburg and Sugarcreek and some of the larger towns.

Also, you will find that most restaurants and bed-and-breakfasts do not allow smoking inside.

Many of the Amish businesses, restaurants, and attractions do accept major credit cards.

A good place to start your trip through the Amish land of Ohio is near the town of Berlin at the Mennonite Information Center. Here you can see a cyclorama, or large circular painting, of the history of the Amish and Mennonite people. The work, which is 10 feet tall and 265 feet long, took 14 years to complete by artist Heinz Gaugel. More of his artwork is displayed at the center. Knowledgeable guides will answer questions about the faith and customs of the area. There is a bookstore and gift shop in the building as well as some large, clean public rest rooms. Admission is charged to see the cyclorama.

Behalt at the Mennonite Information Center   ☎ (330) 893-3192
5798 County Rd. 77 • Berlin, Ohio
Handicapped access: yes

THE AMISH WAY OF LIFE

A close-up look at the Amish lifestyle can be had at an authentic Amish farm, open to the public, just outside of Berlin. The farm consists of a main house, the grandparents' house, barns, and a group of craft shops that have been opened by the present owner. There are also Amish buggy rides available. Admission charged.

Shrock's Amish Farm   ☎ (330) 893-2951
S.R. 39, East • Berlin, Ohio
Handicapped access: steps into some buildings

THE FIRST CHEESE FACTORY

The area's cheese production began in the early 1930s with the opening of Heini's Bunker Hill Cheese Company, the first really large maker of Swiss cheese in the area. Today, the Dauwalder family still operates the business, which now ships cheese all over the world. They offer free tours of the cheese-making operation during the morning hours on weekdays, and have a salesroom where you can have free samples from the more than 50 varieties of cheese that they make and sell here—everything from Swiss to chocolate cheese. That's right, chocolate. It tastes a little like fudge. Heini's also offers a series of shops in its complex that sell fudge, crafts, souvenirs, fresh baked goods, and many other things.

Heini's Bunker Hill Cheese Company   ☎ (330) 893-2131
6005 County Rd. 77 • Berlin, Ohio
Handicapped access: yes

A ROMANTIC HIDEAWAY

In Berlin, tucked away on a back street within walking distance of the main street, is a quaint bed-and-breakfast that offers a unique hideaway for honeymoons, anniversary celebrations, or any special occasion. There are two rooms in the main house and two small cottages that were once carriage barns. The cottages offer cathedral ceilings, floor-to-ceiling fireplaces, four-poster beds with Amish quilts, a whirlpool bath for two with lights, and even a small water-fall! In the morning, the owner discreetly places a tray with a large breakfast on it on a cart outside the door. Reservations are an absolute must here almost anytime.

Donna's Premier Lodging   ☎ (330) 893-3068
East St. • Berlin, Ohio
Handicapped access: yes

TOUR A FORGE

This is the newest attraction in the Amish area. This Pennsylvania-based company has opened a barn-like gift shop and forge on the outskirts of Berlin. They make hammered aluminum and copper plates, trays, dishes, and other metal products. The forge, where the craftsmen do their work, is in the rear of the building and is open for tours. There is also a small museum in the building with hammered aluminum products from the past and also the world's largest Amish buggy. Tour groups are welcome.

Wendell August Forge   ☎ (330) 893-3713
U.S. 62 • Berlin, Ohio
Handicapped access: yes

A NICE MOTEL

Most of the motels and inns in this area are sparkling clean, and many offer wonderful pastoral views of the Amish countryside. On the outskirts of Berlin there is a small family-run motel that has been in business since before the tourist rush began. It sits on a hillside overlooking some Amish farms below. The rooms are large and offer cable TV, good-sized bathrooms, and comfortable beds. At the height of the tourist season reservations are usually required, and they are a good idea any time of year.

Berlin Village Inn   ☎ (800) 869-7571
S.R. 39, West • Berlin, Ohio
Handicapped access: yes

A POOL, A RESTAURANT, A MOTEL

While you don't find many places to stay in Amish country that offer big-city amenities like swimming pools and exercise rooms, there are exceptions. On the outskirts of Berlin, operated by the same folks who run the Amish Farm, is a motel-restaurant complex that measures up to those in many big cities. The motel, in one building, is built on the edge of a farmer's meadow where you can usually find cows and horses grazing. Each of the rooms has a small balcony, cable TV, and a large bathroom and bedroom. Next door is the restaurant, with a glass wall that overlooks the pasture. A fireplace dominates the main portion of the dining room. The specialty is Amish-style cooking with fresh baked goods. On the other side of the motel is a fitness center that is open to motel guests. It includes exercise equipment, a spa and swimming pool, and a health bar.

The Amish Country Inn & Dutch Harvest Restaurant   ☎ (330) 893-3000
S.R. 39 West • Berlin, Ohio
Handicapped access: yes

A WAY TO TAKE AMISH COUNTRY HOME WITH YOU

If you would like some beautiful photos of the Amish and their countryside, watch for the work of local resident Doyle Yoder in the gift stores, craft shops, and restaurants in the area. Doyle was born and raised with the Amish. Their trust of him is apparent in the sensitive photos he takes in every season of the year. He has also contributed to a large photo book that shows the Amish communities across the United States. It, too, is available in most shops in the region. For a catalog of Doyle's work and other books and pictures he offers, write to:

Doyle Yoder, Photographer   ☎
Amish Country Calendar, P.O. Box 424 • Berlin, Ohio

ONE TANK TIP #8

Eating on the Road

Carry a small cooler with drinks and snacks in it on long road trips. This saves money, lets you have an impromptu picnic along the road, and provides emergency food when it's late and you don't feel like looking for a restaurant.

29 **The Amish Capital**

Millersburg, Ohio, could easily be called the capital of the Amish region. It is the county seat of Holmes County, where the vast majority of the world's Amish live. In fact the county courthouse has a hitching rail for Amish horses on a street out front.

They also once had parking meters for the horses, just like they did on other streets for automobiles. Sadly, the parking meters, which used to make such a wonderful photographic opportunity for tourists, are now gone, and I believe it is my fault.

Some years ago I noticed that while police were ticketing parked automobiles, I did not see any tickets on the Amish buggies that were also parked at expired meters.

I went to see Millersburg chief of police Darryl Weiss and asked him why it was that while motorists seemed to be getting tickets, the Amish were not.

"That's not so," he said. "We ticket the Amish, the problem is tracking down just who the horse and buggy belongs to."

He went on to point out an obvious fact I had missed. The Amish are not required to license their buggies, or horses for that matter, like motorists are. So when a police officer goes to write a parking ticket for an overdue meter, and the culprit is a dark horse and a black buggy, how does he identify it? Especially if five other practically identical horses and buggies are parked legally right beside it!

I granted that the chief had a problem.

"How do you handle the situation?" I asked.

"We usually just write the ticket and leave the license number and make of car section blank or write 'horse' where it says 'car,'" he said. "Then we hope they will come in, or send in the fine."

"Do they?" I asked.

Chief Weiss paused.

"Sometimes they do, sometimes they don't," he finally answered. "I guess it's really not fair to motorists and we ought to do something about it."

A couple of months later the parking meters were gone all over the downtown.

Was it because of my inquiry, or was it just the village fathers reacting to the arrival of a large discount store on the outskirts of town with an effort to keep local customers downtown?

I guess I'll never know, but I sort of miss the sight of the horses tied to the parking meters at the courthouse.

SPIRITS AND TRADITION

You can find both at the Hotel Millersburg, built more than a century and a half ago. It has recently been modernized and is one of the few places in Holmes County where you can have an alcoholic drink with your dinner.

The governor of Ohio has stayed here, as well as other celebrities. The rooms offer cable TV, large modern bathrooms, and the convenience of being in downtown Millersburg. Enjoy outdoor dining and entertainment on the patio between Memorial Day and Labor Day.

Hotel Millersburg   ☎ (330) 674-1457
35 W. Jackson St. · Millersburg, Ohio
Handicapped access: steps to second floor

A REALLY BIG ICE-CREAM CONE

If you like ice cream, I mean lots of ice cream, we have a store for you. It's a small grocery store in downtown Millersburg where they don't sell ice-cream cones by the dip. They sell them by the pound! A "double" contains nearly a pound of ice cream, and that's a really big ice-cream cone.

The Grocery Bag   ☎ (330) 674-0833
189 N. Clay St. · Millersburg, Ohio
Handicapped access: yes

AN INTRODUCTION TO THE COUNTY

A publication provides maps, recipes, and stories of the Amish area, as well as some beautiful photographs. If you plan to spend any time in the area or just enjoy country stories and photos, you might want to subscribe to it. It's published by a local couple, Fran and Abe Mast, who grew up in the area and know just about everybody.

The Holmes County Traveler Magazine   ☎ (330) 674-2300
County Rd. 623 · Millersburg, Ohio

A FIREPLACE IN THE BEDROOM

If you are looking for a really private place to spend the night here, try a bed-and-breakfast. In Millersburg, a former Victorian home that once belonged to the local doctor has been converted into a bed-and-breakfast. One of the bedrooms has its own fireplace and private bath and is beautifully furnished. The tearoom is open for light lunches, teas, and special occasions by reservation.

Bigham House of Millersburg Bed-and-Breakfast ☎ (330) 674-2404
154 S. Washington St. • Millersburg, Ohio
Handicapped access: steps into house and to second floor

WATCH IT MADE RIGHT BEFORE YOUR EYES

This woolen mill on the outskirts of Millersburg has been here for over a century, and the same family has operated it nearly that long. You are invited to drop in any day they are in operation and watch wool being turned into rich, colorful rugs. They also have a store where they sell wool clothing and other wool products.

Rastetter's Woolen Mill ☎ (330) 674-2103
5802 S.R. 39 • Millersburg, Ohio
Handicapped access: narrow aisles in shop

A DIFFERENT KIND OF PLACE TO STAY

The Inn at Honey Run is not your ordinary Amish Country inn. To be sure, it has Amish help and is located far off the main road in the center of Amish farmland, but the similarities end there. Owner Marge Stock, formerly of Cleveland, has built a hideaway that attracts the likes of the governor and his wife when they are trying to escape the pressures of public life.

The inn itself cannot be seen from the highway. It is hidden among tall trees. The menu reflects the local cuisine but also includes farm-raised trout, steaks, and other country delicacies prepared in original recipes. Usually reservations are needed for both lunch and dinner at the inn.

As for the sleeping accommodations, they too are original. Several sleeping units have been built into the side of a hill (they look like a giant beehive from below). There are beautifully furnished guest houses on top of the hill nestled in groves of trees, each with fireplace, kitchen, bedrooms, and all the modern amenities. The inn is truly an out-of-the-ordinary place to spend a night or a weekend in Amish country.

The Inn at Honey Run   ☎ (800) 468-6639
6920 County Rd. 203 · Millersburg, Ohio
Handicapped access: yes

THE PEWTERWARE MAKER OF MILLERSBURG

There are only five places left in the entire United States where you can actually watch a Master Pewterware maker spin pewter. Millersburg, Ohio, is one of them. David N. Three Feathers Jones and his apprentice, Willa Hollingsworth, operate Three Feathers Pewter, across from the historic courthouse in downtown Millersburg.

Jones apprenticed himself to Master Pewterer Carl Steen many years ago to learn the rare art of spinning pewter. He opened his pewter business in 1984. He says he got the name "Three Feathers" when he was adopted by the Moon Society of the Shawnee Nation of Native Americans. Today in his gallery in downtown Millersburg, tourists can watch Jones and his apprentice spin pewter into fine pieces of jewelry or housewares that look like instant antiques.

Three Feathers Pewter   ☎ (330) 674-0404
12 East Jackson St. · Millersburg, Ohio
Handicapped access: yes

ONE TANK TIP #9

Try a Bed-and-Breakfast

If motels are full and you didn't make reservations, ask the clerk for a list of local bed-and-breakfasts. Often they have vacancies when motels near main roads are full.

30 Back Roads of Ohio's Amish Land

It was a foggy spring morning. It had rained almost all night, and now the mist of morning was just starting to burn away as the sun teased us with the promise of a balmy day.

Videographer Bill West and I had driven to this gravel road in the Doughty Valley, east of Millersburg, to do a report on what I called an "Amish motel": a collection of log cabins on a hillside operated as a campground by an Amish family. The cabins had just been completed a few weeks earlier, and we had convinced the publicity-shy Amish owners that it would be good for their business if we showed their new enterprise. We had also promised not to take any pictures of the owners.

The cabins were scattered down a hillside that overlooked the Doughty Creek, which flows through the valley. Across the valley, you could make out the stainless steel storage tanks at the Guggisberg Cheese Company, just now emerging from the morning fog.

I stepped out of our car and immediately noticed a strong odor of horse manure. But being in Amish Country, where horses are the main means of transportation, I gave it little thought. Bill was setting up his camera as I walked to the edge of the hillside to get a good look at the cabins. The wet ground seemed to be covered with straw. I stepped onto the steep path that led towards the cabins, and I felt my feet start to slip. I threw up my arms to regain my balance, but then both feet went out from underneath me and I landed on my back and started to slide, through the mud and straw, down the hill.

When I finally came to a stop about 30 feet down the hillside, I realized where the smell of horse manure had been coming from. They had just seeded the hillside and spread fresh manure on it for fertilizer. I was now coated from the top of my head to the bottom of my heels with a mixture of horse dung, straw, and wet mud.

Videographer West and an Amish woman came skidding down the hill to help. They helped me to my feet, both trying—not too successfully—to smother their laughter as I stood up, mud and dung dripping from my hair, my back, and my legs.

"Where's the bathroom?" I asked the Amish lady.

She covered her mouth with one hand to disguise a smile and

used the other to point to a small wooden building at the bottom of the hill.

"There it is," she said, "but there's no running water here."

"Where's the nearest place I can clean myself up?" I asked.

She pointed across the valley towards the Guggisberg Cheese Company's store.

I started walking up the hill towards our newscruiser. As I approached the door, Bill West jumped in front of me and said, "Where are you going?"

I explained that I was going to get in the car and have him drive me down to the cheese company so I could use their modern bathroom.

"You're not going to get in my newscruiser like that!" he said, refusing to budge.

"Well, how am I supposed to get over there then?" I replied in a testy voice.

He pointed to the hood of his car.

A few minutes later, clinging to the hood of the newscruiser, spread-eagled across the car like some large animal bagged in a hunt, I was driven down the hill and across the valley, past startled Amish families in their buggies, to the cheese factory, where I was finally able to wash up.

As to how you rent those cabins, most of the Amish don't have telephones. But if you call on a Monday morning, they station one of the Amish youngsters at a pay telephone across the street from the cabins to take messages about reservations. Just let it ring a long time, in case he has decided to wander down the road to explore the ditch.

Actually, the cabins, while primitive, are quite nice. They offer a wood-burning stove, kerosene lamps, cookware and bedding for a family of at least four, and furniture for a very reasonable price. And, at the top of the hill, there is a non-electric bakery.

Countryside Camper's Paradise   ☎ (330) 893-3002 Mon 8:30 a.m.–6 p.m.
4280 Township Rd. 356, Rte. 4 • Millersburg, Ohio
Handicapped access: gravel path and steps into cabins

GUGGISBERG CHEESE FACTORY

Just across the valley is the place where Baby Swiss cheese was created. They make it Monday through Friday, and you're invited to watch in the morning, as well as visit their store and purchase some to take home.

Guggisberg Cheese   ☎ (330) 893-2500
S.R. 557 • Millersburg, Ohio
Handicapped access: yes

Guggisberg Cheese

CHALET IN THE VALLEY RESTAURANT

Across the street from the cheese factory is another of the Guggisberg family enterprises: an authentic Swiss chalet that serves Swiss, Austrian, and Amish foods. There is also a bakery on the premises. During tourist season this is a very busy place, and the wait for a table can be up to an hour at lunchtime.

Chalet in the Valley   ☎ (330) 893-2550
5060 SR 557 • Millersburg, Ohio
Handicapped access: yes

SLEIGH RIDES AND HAYRIDES

Another enterprise of the Guggisberg family is just up the road, where son Eric and his wife, Julie, have opened an inn. It offers whirlpool bathtubs in some rooms and includes packages that give you and a loved one a horse-drawn sleigh ride (when there is snow on the ground). In warmer weather, a horse-drawn Amish buggy takes you on a tour of the surrounding farms.

Guggisberg Swiss Inn/Amish Country Riding Stables   ☎ (877) 467-9477
5025 S.R. 557 • Charm, Ohio
Handicapped access: yes

A CHARMING BED AND BREAKFAST

An Amish and Mennonite family operate a bed-and-breakfast on State Route 557. The building is new and set back from the road among the trees, with a great view of the pasture, where cows and horses graze. The building is air-conditioned and has electricity. Each room has a private, modern bath, and many of the quilts on the beds were made by family members. The breakfast is more like an Amish feast. If you are a big eater, you will love this place. There are 15 rooms, and reservations are a must!

The Charm Countryview Inn Bed-and-Breakfast   ☎ (330) 893-3003
S.R. 557 • Charm, Ohio
Handicapped access: yes

A HILLTOP BED AND BREAKFAST

This is also a brand new bed-and-breakfast, built on the highest spot in Holmes County and offering a breathtaking view of the Amish countryside. The owners raise miniature horses and goats. Each of the nicely appointed bedrooms has a private bath. The breakfast served here is no wimpy "continental-style" juice and roll; it's a full-blown Amish breakfast that includes homemade rolls and eggs and ham and other things. As at most popular inns, you must make reservations here well in advance.

Millerhaus Bed-and-Breakfast   ☎ (330) 893-3602
3135 County Rd. 135 • Charm, Ohio
Handicapped access: limited

A FOUR-DIAMOND INN

In Walnut Creek, the Dutch Corporation, which owns the original Amish-style restaurant in town, has built a beautiful hilltop inn that recently received an automobile club's prestigious four-diamond award. Some of the beautifully decorated suites have whirlpool baths for two, balconies overlooking Amish farms, and a country ambiance that is hard to describe until you stay there. The inn is very busy, and reservations are a must.

Carlisle Village Inn ☎ (330) 893-3636
4949 Walnut St. (State Rte. 515) • Walnut Creek, Ohio
Handicapped access: yes

SMELLS GOOD AND TASTES GOOD

There really is a Mrs. Kaufman, who made the Mrs. Kaufman's Jams and Jellies that you find across Ohio at farm markets and stores. Her daughter continues the business and still makes the jams and jellies, small batch by small batch, in a modest building at the rear of her home. Stop in when she's working and you can watch. There's no charge for the wonderful smell.

Mrs. Kaufman's Jams ☎ (330) 893-3278
3483 S.R. 39 West • Walnut Creek, Ohio
Handicapped access: steps into building

A LOOK AT AN AMISH HOME

If you are curious about the lifestyle of these hardworking people who shun modern life, you can peek behind their curtains without invading their privacy at Yoder's Amish Home, near Walnut Creek. Eli Yoder was raised Amish, and many of his family are still members of the community. The home and farm they have opened to the public was originally owned by another Amish family, and many of the guides who work at the farm today are Amish. You can see both an old-fashioned Amish home and a more modern one that includes many non-electric appliances that may surprise you—including freezers and refrigerators. Rides in authentic Amish buggies are available, and locally made quilts and crafts are for sale.

Yoder's Amish Home ☎ (330) 893-2541
S.R. 515 • Walnut Creek, Ohio
Handicapped access: yes, but gravel paths and steps into homes

SOUTHEAST OHIO

31 Frank Takes a Ride

It was a brutally cold winter day. The temperature was hovering near the zero mark. It was perfect weather for a ride on Ohio's longest and fastest toboggan slide.

East Sparta, Ohio, south of Canton, is home to Bear Creek Camp Grounds. Once the temperature goes down near the 40-degree mark, Bear Creek is able to start the refrigeration equipment that freezes the toboggan chute. The chute stretches for nearly a half-mile. You ride a truck to the top of a 250-foot-high hill at the back of the property, where a small two-story building is located. On the second floor is a platform that stretches out over the chute. You place your toboggan on this platform and then, when you are ready, an attendant drops the front of the platform, plunging you down one story onto the frozen chute. During the ride to the bottom of the 250-foot slope, you reach speeds of up to 70 miles per hour.

In case you are unable to stop when you reach the end of the chute, there is a 30-foot-long bed of straw and, beyond that, a stack of baled straw to stop runaway toboggans.

This is, quite simply, one of the most exciting outdoor rides in Ohio.

On the day we were taping our story, sending me up and down the toboggan run, we were alerted to a birthday celebration that was about to take place.

An elderly gentleman named Frank was about to take his first ride on the icy chute to celebrate his 90th birthday.

I asked Frank if he objected to our taping his ride. He did not. I asked why he had chosen such an unusual way to mark his 90th year.

"I've always wanted to slide down that hill," he said, adding, "I thought I had better do it pretty soon or forget it."

Frank also pointed out that he wasn't going down the hill alone. His neighbor was going to ride with him. His neighbor was 87!

We watched as the pair was trucked to the top of the hill and their toboggan carried into the little shed and up to the second floor.

By straining our eyes we could just see Frank and his neighbor climb aboard the toboggan, and we started our camera rolling.

The toboggan dropped and came flashing down the hill. The track was exceptionally slick that day, and they reached top speed quickly.

When they passed our camera position, nearly three-quarters of the way down the chute, they whipped by us at such a great speed we were unable to focus on them.

We wheeled around just in time to see them reach the end of the chute, slice through the 30 feet of straw, and slam head-on into a pile of baled straw. Both men tumbled off the toboggan.

Everyone was running towards them. Frank's neighbor was getting up, but Frank was still not moving. He was just lying there on his side, beside the capsized toboggan.

Several people were calling to him.

"Frank! Frank! Are you all right?"

Frank opened his eyes and said, "Is it over yet?"

Later I asked Frank if he was planning to take another ride.

"Not until I turn 100!" he answered.

Toboggans run when weather permits

Bear Creek Resort   ☎ (330) 484-3901
3232 Downing St., S.W. • East Sparta, Ohio
Handicapped access: steps to launching area

BED AND BREAKFAST IN A HISTORIC CABIN

For a spot to spend the night in this area and a dinner you won't soon forget, head south on I-77 to historic Zoar. One of the oldest cabins in the village, Cowger House Number 9, is a unique bed-and-breakfast that offers not only the charm of a frontier cabin bedroom but also a private bathroom. The real treat here, for an additional cost, is the special fireside dinner that the owners put on by reservation only. Not only is the food excellent, but there is also entertainment that I can't tell you about without spoiling the surprise. I will tell you that if you enjoy American history you will be telling your friends about this place.

Cowger House #9   ☎ (800) 874-3542
4th St. • Zoar, Ohio
Handicapped access: yes to one building; steps to some rooms in other buildings

OHIO'S UNKNOWN SOLDIER

Ohio had only one Revolutionary War fort, and it was at Bolivar, just up the road from Zoar. Here you can find the remains of Fort Laurens. The Ohio Historical Society has a building on the site where you can see a slide presentation on the fort and its story. Nearby is a tomb that holds the remains of one of the defenders of the fort. His body was discovered about 20 years ago when a new driveway was being built at the site.

He was later reinterred in a granite tomb as Ohio's "unknown soldier." (Open seasonally)

Fort Laurens State Memorial   ☎ (800) 283-8914
11067 Ft. Laurens Rd. (County Rd. 102)   •   Bolivar, Ohio
Handicapped access: yes

A WILDERNESS CANOE EXPERIENCE

If you have ever planned to take the family canoeing on a hot summer's day and found the river looking like I-71 at rush hour, you may want to try this canoe livery near Bolivar. It has been around for nearly a quarter of a century. They rent only 50 canoes and so don't crowd the river like many other canoe liveries do. This does mean waiting for a canoe at times, but the experience you and the family have and the peace and quiet of the river will be well worth it. By the way, the initials stand for Nature Trails Rental. They offer some special events, like Halloween haunted trails and a Christmas decoration tour of area homes when it's too cold to go canoeing.

NTR Canoe Livery   ☎ (330) 874-2002
11358 SR 212 (just east of I-77)   •   Bolivar, Ohio
Handicapped access: yes

32 Ohio's First City

Marietta was Ohio's first city, part of the Northwest Territory leading to the western frontier. It was settled because of its location at the confluence of the Muskingham and Ohio rivers.

Today it wears its antiquity like a proud badge, still a small river city though it has been a favorite with tourists for years.

One man responsible for putting Marietta on the tourist maps is Captain Jim Sands of the *Valley Gem* sternwheeler. For many years, his has been one of the last operating paddle-wheel boats in Ohio.

Valley Gem Sternwheeler

The *Valley Gem* gives visitors a chance to see what life on the river was like, to experience the slow, regal travel of the great sternwheelers. Captain Sands also takes the ship up the Muskingham and through the 150-year-old hand-operated locks at the Muskingham River dam. It's a wonderful trip on an autumn day, with both sides of the river painted in fall colors. He offers dinner cruises and even performs wedding ceremonies on his boat. Former president George Bush, former Ohio governor George Voinovich, and other notables have taken turns at the wheel in the pilothouse high atop the boat.

A year ago, Captain Sands's efforts to bring tourists to his river-front city paid off. Because the number of passengers he was serving grew each year, he traded in the old *Valley Gem* for a brand-new ship nearly twice its size. Today, the new *Valley Gem* continues to explore the Ohio and Muskingham rivers on a year-round basis with daily cruises in the spring and summer and charter dinner cruises during the winter months.

***Valley Gem* Sternwheeler** ☎ (740) 373-7862
Docked at Washington St. Landing • Marietta, Ohio
Mailing address: 123 Strecker Hill, Marietta, OH 45750
Handicapped access: yes

A COLA MUSEUM

This museum is a tribute to a Marietta man who loved Coca Cola so much that he built a museum to his favorite drink. You'll find early Coke advertising, signs, soft-drink machines, and even ice-cold Coke—still in bottles. There is a gift shop where you can buy replicas of early advertising signs and other Coke memorabilia.

Marietta Soda Museum ☎ (740) 376-2653
118 Maple St. • Marietta, Ohio
Handicapped access: steps into building

FLAGS AND POLES

There is a unique business in this river town: a shop that sells nothing but flags and flagpoles. You can buy anything from a miniature American flag for a parade all the way up to a 40-foot aluminum pole and all the hardware to get Old Glory flying in front of your home or business.

American Flags and Poles ☎ (800) 262-3524
276 Front St. (Rte. 7) • Marietta, Ohio
Handicapped access: yes

A RIVERBOAT THEATER

The Becky Thatcher Riverboat Theater started life as a working sternwheeler. When many of the old riverboats began heading for the scrap dealers after World War II, some far-sighted Marietta residents saw the possibility of re-creating a bit of river history by converting this old sternwheeler into a permanently docked theater and restaurant. Today, the theater offers authentic riverboat melodramas, as well as musical shows, during the summer and autumn tourist seasons. The restaurant on the upper deck offers fine foods and a wonderful view of the Muskingham River The restaurant is closed on Sunday, year round; theater is seasonal.

Becky Thatcher Restaurant and Show Boat
☎ (740) 373-4130 restaurant; (740) 373-6033 theater
237 Front St. • Marietta, Ohio
Handicapped access: yes

GARDEN GLOBE FACTORY

If you have ever lusted after one of those silver garden balls that sit atop a birdbath—you know, the kind a fortune teller might have—we've found the last place in America that makes them. You can buy seconds right here at the factory. Closed Saturday and Sunday.

Marietta Silver Globe Manufacturing Company   ☎ (740) 373-4951
State Rte. 550 (Pinehurst Rd.) • Marietta, Ohio
Handicapped access: busy factory, gravel driveway

SLEEP ON A STERNWHEELER

This is the only place in Ohio where you can actually sleep overnight on an authentic sternwheeler. The *Claire* is a retired work boat that has been converted into a floating bed-and-breakfast. However, because of insurance requirements, when guests are on board the ship must remain docked. The boat offers three staterooms with a shared bath and nicely appointed living room (or main salon, as the riverboaters like to say). In the morning, you troop off the boat and up the dock to the nearby Levee House Restaurant, also operated by the boat's owner, where you get your breakfast.

***Claire* Sternwheeler Boat Bed-and-Breakfast**   ☎ (740) 374-2233
127 Ohio St. • Marietta, Ohio
Handicapped access: steps in and out of rooms on boat

LEVEE HOUSE CAFE AND RESTAURANT

This former warehouse has stood for more than a century facing the Ohio River. The current owner renovated it and made it into a unique restaurant specializing in gourmet cuisine. An herb garden right outside the front door is used by the chef in the summer months to add fresh flavor to his dishes. Also, in good weather, the tables on the patio are a great place to have a glass of wine and watch a sunset on the Ohio River.

Levee House Cafe and Restaurant   ☎ (740) 374-2233
127 Ohio St. • Marietta, Ohio
Handicapped access: yes

A PASTA FACTORY

You can watch gourmet pasta being made in this small riverfront factory. The pasta is shipped all over the U.S. and has been a favorite of celebrities, including the late Frank Sinatra. The factory store offers all the different varieties made here, as well as sauces to go with them, and recipes.

Rossi Pasta Factory   ☎ (740) 373-5155
114 Greene St. • Marietta, Ohio
Handicapped access: yes

CAMPUS MARTIUS MUSEUM AND OHIO RIVER MUSEUM

The Campus Martius Museum houses the home of Rufus Putnam, one of the founders of Marietta. It also has a good collection of exhibits on the early history of native Americans and later migrations of people into and within Ohio. The Ohio River Museum, a block away, is a treasure trove of Ohio River steamboat history. Both are operated by the Ohio Historical Society.

Ohio River and Campus Martius Museums   ☎ (800) 860-0145
Washington and Second St. • Marietta, Ohio
Handicapped access: yes

From My Mailbag...

Dear Mr. Zurcher,

You forgot to mention on your show about Columbus that they offer tours of the Anheuser-Busch Beer Company. You must have Anheuser's disease.

--Disturbed in Wooster

33 A Train Ride into the Past

The entire town of Sugarcreek is decorated like a Swiss village, with a facade on each business resembling that of a chalet. Even the pay phone standing on a downtown corner looks like a miniature chalet. There is a small, neat, brick railroad station here. But unlike the abandoned stations of other small towns, this one plays host to thousands of passengers each year. This is the headquarters of the Ohio Central Railroad.

The Ohio Central Railroad is not your ordinary tourist train. It's an honest-to-gosh working small-line railroad that hauls freight from these small towns out to the Conrail and the Chessie System lines. And it also offers passenger tours. This passenger service has attracted upward of 100,000 visitors to ride the train over seven miles of track to Baltic, Ohio, and then return. It isn't very far, but in those seven miles the locomotive passes through picturesque Amish farms as the history of the valley is recited by friendly conductors.

Unfortunately, back in 1998, some people in the village weren't happy with the train. Smoke, dirt, and the sheer number of people that swarmed to ride upset some local folks. Officials at Ohio Central were unhappy that the village did not do more to welcome the customers the train attracted. The differences continued to grow until the decision was made to stop the train service at the end of the 1998 season.

But today it's back and operating daily during summer and fall—except on Sundays. For information, contact:

Ohio Central Railroad   ☎ (330) 852-4676
111 Factory St. NE • Sugarcreek, Ohio
Handicapped access: steps into railroad cars

A MUSEUM OF CHEESE

They celebrate cheese in this town because it is one of the staples of life here. This tiny museum on the main street shows, in specially prepared rooms, how early cheese-making was done. It also offers a peek into the past of this community with a nice display of local memorabilia and early vehicles.

Alpine Hills Museum   ☎ (330) 852-4113
106 W. Main St. • Sugarcreek, Ohio
Handicapped access: yes

Alpine Hills Museum

SLEEP IN A BARN

You can literally sleep in a barn here in Sugarcreek, albeit a luxurious barn. Sitting on a hilltop just outside of town is a bed-and-breakfast located in what was once a working Amish barn. Where hay was once stored, today there are rooms with cable TV, small balconies, modern bathrooms, and—are you ready for this—satin sheets on the bed. The bed-and-breakfast also offers Sunday -night dinner to its guests because most of the other restaurants in the area are not open on Sunday.

The Barn Bed-and-Breakfast   ☎ (330) 852-2337
560 Sugarcreek Rd. • Sugarcreek, Ohio
Handicapped access: steps to some rooms

A CARVER'S DELIGHT

A member of a famous carving family has brought his talents to the Sugarcreek area. David Warther, grandson of famed Dover carver Ernest "Moony" Warther, has opened his studio to the public. David has dedicated his life to the history of sailing ships, much as his grandfather did to the history of steam engines. David already has completed a large number of exquisite ivory ships that trace the beginnings of ships powered by wind—from Biblical times to the present. The models are not for sale, but all are displayed to be enjoyed by visitors.

David Warther Carvings   ☎ (330) 852-3455
1387 Old Rte. 39 · Sugarcreek, Ohio
Handicapped access: yes

A NEW CHRISTMAS TRADITION

A wonderful Christmas experience for children is now available in Southeast Ohio. The Polar Express, a train trip based on the book by the same name written and illustrated by Chris Van Allsburg, is now running each holiday season out of Dennison's historic train station. Children and their parents take the evening ride in December and are encouraged to wear pajamas as they set off on a mythical trip to the North Pole in search of Santa Claus. The train cars are decorated with Christmas wreaths and lights, and "elves" are on board to pass out hot chocolate and lead the kids in caroling on the first leg of the trip to discover Santa. On the way home, Santa rides with the youngsters and listens to their holiday desires. The program has been an absolute sellout for several years on the Cuyahoga Valley Railroad in Northeast Ohio. It's expected to do he same here, so get your reservations early.

The Polar Express   ☎ (866) 850-4676
The Ohio Central Railroad · Sugarcreek, Ohio

FOOD THE AMISH WAY

There are several Amish-style restaurants in and around Sugarcreek. This one is operated by the same firm that owns Der Dutchman in Walnut Creek. They serve the traditional Amish fare of beef, turkey, and ham with lots of mashed potatoes, gravy, and stuffing, as well as a large salad bar, homemade bread, and pies—all for a reasonable price. Most everything is made fresh each day in the kitchen. There is also a bakery in-house so you can take home some of those Amish goodies. Closed on Sundays.

Dutch Valley Restaurant   ☎ (330) 852-4627
S.R. 39, East • Sugarcreek, Ohio
Handicapped access: yes

Sugarcreek, Ohio

CRAFTS AND MORE CRAFTS

An old hardware store on the edge of town has taken on new life as an outlet for local artists and craftspeople. More than 130 of them are represented here, by everything from homemade wooden pitchforks to intricate Amish quilts. There are paintings, knick-knacks, and even a sturdy children's farm wagon, crafted by an Amish entrepreneur who makes his living building horse-drawn manure spreaders for his neighbors. You can shop here every day but Sunday. Credit cards are welcome, as is cash.

Artisan's Mercantile of Sugarcreek   ☎ (330) 852-2456
110 Andreas Dr. • Sugarcreek, Ohio
Handicapped access: yes

34 The Longest Ride

One of my favorite Ohio secrets is a tiny, community-operated amusement park tucked away in a city park that offers what must be the longest merry-go-round ride in America. Tuscora Park in New Philadelphia has had a tradition for generations of giving youngsters their money's worth when they climb aboard the carousel at the park. The ride usually lasts five minutes or more. The folks who operate it say that in recent years they have started cutting back on the time because after going around and around for five minutes, many youngsters got so dizzy they became sick to their stomachs!

The carousel is a Spillman, made in New York, and it has been in constant use at Tuscora Park since 1940.

In addition to the merry-go-round, the park also offers several other attractions, including a Ferris wheel, miniature train, small roller coaster, and some kiddie rides. The park also holds the city's swimming pool and picnic area. Open May–Labor Day.

Tuscora Park ☎ (330) 343-4644
161 Tuscora Ave., N.W. • New Philadelphia, Ohio
Handicapped access: yes

TRUMPET IN THE LAND

This distinguished outdoor drama was among the first outdoor theater presentations in Ohio. Thousands have come to an amphitheater just on the outskirts of New Philadelphia to see the story of Moravian missionary David Zeisberger and his attempts to keep peaceful Native Americans out of the fighting between the British and the American colonists during the Revolutionary War. His efforts ended in a tragic massacre of the Native Americans. The play runs from mid June through late August each summer.

Trumpet in the Land / White Savage Outdoor Dramas
☎ (330) 364-5111
Trumpet Dr. (off SR 250) • New Philadelphia, Ohio
Handicapped access: yes

Trumpet in the Land Outdoor Drama

SCHOENBRUNN VILLAGE

After you see *Trumpet in the Land*, you may want to see some of the places that figured prominently in the drama. One of them, Schoenbrunn Village, is nearby. This was the village founded by David Zeisberger and his Christian Indians. The homes, the school, and the church have all been re-created. Costumed interpreters tell the village's story when it is open (during the summer months, from Memorial Day until Labor Day).

Schoenbrunn Village   ☎ (800) 752-2711
S.R. 259 · New Philadelphia, Ohio
Handicapped access: yes

GNADENHUTTEN

This is probably the town with the most-often-mispronounced name in the state. It was in Gnadenhutten that the tragic incident happened on which the play *Trumpet in the Land* was based. In 1782, an American militia massacred 96 Christian Indians because they refused to take sides in the Revolutionary War. Today, you can see the mass grave as well as a replica of the cabin where the killing occurred.

Gnadenhutten Historical Society ☎ (740) 254-4143
352 S. Cherry St. • Gnadenhutten, Ohio
Handicapped access: yes

HOME OF THE "KING OF HOLLYWOOD"

He was known as the "King of Hollywood," but Clark Gable was born in the middle of the Ohio coalfields in Cadiz, Ohio.

Just recently opened, this small, two-story frame home is an exact replica of Gable's original home, which stood near downtown Cadiz but was torn down many years ago. Pictures of Gable and his family adorn the walls. You can see the small upstairs bedroom where the future star was born. In a nearby bedroom is a pair of pajamas from his Hollywood days, as well as correspondence between Gable and former president Dwight D. Eisenhower. Outside, Gable's 1954 Cadillac sits in the driveway. It is said that he was driving this very car when he had his first heart attack.

In the basement is a small theater where a short film is shown about Gable's life in Cadiz and his career in Hollywood.

At present there is no elevator to take handicapped visitors to the second-floor museum or the basement theater area, but officials for the museum said one is planned.

Clark Gable's Birthplace Gift Shop and Museum ☎ (740) 942-4989
138 Charleston St. • Cadiz, Ohio
Handicapped access: no

THE WARTHER LEGACY

In the 87 years of his life, Ernest "Moony" Warther left more than 60 intricate wood carvings as his legacy. Warther, who went no further than the second grade in school, did the carvings with no formal training, yet some of the foremost carvers in the world have proclaimed him "the Master Carver."

He carved many things, but his most famous carvings show the history of steam engines, including a made-to-scale, eight-foot-long replica of Abraham Lincoln's funeral train done entirely in ebony and ivory. He was working on his 64th carving when he died in 1973.

Today, Warther's sons and grandsons carry on the tradition he started, and his carvings are still on display in the family museum.

Warther's Carving Museum ☎ (330) 343-7513
331 Karl Ave. • Dover, Ohio
Handicapped access: yes

Warther Carving Museum

From My Mailbag...

Dear Mr. Zurcher,

I am writing to complain about the directions you gave on TV. You said I should take Interstate 77 from Cleveland but you didn't tell us where Interstate 77 is.

--Lost in Parma

35 The Ohio Valley

If there is a bit of a riverboat gambler in you, if you love country music, if you like the beauty of hills and rivers, then where Ohio meets West Virginia is the place for you.

We'll start just across the river in Wheeling. Located here are the legendary Capitol Theater and *Jamboree U.S.A.*, a program of country music that has been broadcast for more than 70 years on radio station WWVA and is second only to Nashville's Grand Ole Opry in longevity. Saturday nights find some of the top names in country music gracing the stage in downtown Wheeling.

Jamboree U.S.A. ☎ (800) 624-5456 or (304) 232-1170
Capitol Music Hall
1015 Main St. · Wheeling, West Virginia
Handicapped access: yes

HERE COMES SPUNKY

For the gambler, there is Wheeling Island, in the middle of the Ohio River. Here, the greyhounds run year round. This is also the home of one of West Virginia's first electronic gambling casinos. However, don't go looking for roulette wheels or dice tables; offered instead are more than 300 electronic machines that play blackjack, keno, and poker. You must be at least 18 years old to enter the casino, which is open every day—even when the dog track is not.

The track clubhouse has a restaurant where you can dine while watching and betting on the dog races.

Wheeling Downs Racetrack & Gaming Center ☎ (877) 946-4373
Wheeling Island · Wheeling, West Virginia
Handicapped access: yes

WEST VIRGINIA'S INDEPENDENCE HALL

Before 1863 there was no state of West Virginia. All the land that touched the Ohio River in that area belonged to the state of Virginia. Then came the War between the States. In 1861, Virginia had seceded from the Union, leaving the Confederacy on Ohio's doorstep. Virginians loyal to the Union petitioned Washington to let them secede from Virginia. Today, the hall where the conventions creating the new state were held is a restored National Historic Landmark and museum focusing on West Virginia history and culture. Open daily from 10 a.m. until 4 p.m.

West Virginia Independence Hall   ☎ (304) 238-1300
Civil War Historic Site and Museum
1528 Market St. · Wheeling, West Virginia
Handicapped access: yes

OGLEBAY RESORT

One of the truly beautiful areas of West Virginia, Oglebay Resort, has something for just about everyone in the family. There are three professional golf courses, a mountaintop lodge and cottages, West Virginia's only zoo, hiking trails, beautiful gardens, museums, paddleboats, swimming pools ... and the list goes on.

During the Christmas holidays, more than one million lights illuminate this mountaintop resort, and each evening thousands of cars and buses from three states roll up and down the resort roads.

Oglebay Resort   ☎ (800) 624-6988
S.R. 88 · Wheeling, West Virginia
Handicapped access: yes

RENT A CAMP

Back on the Ohio side of the river there is a unique state park where you can try camping without spending much money. Barkcamp State Park's rent-a-camp program provides a family with a walled tent for the night, along with cots, lantern, cooler, cook stove, picnic table, and even a broom to clean up with. All you have to bring along is your blankets and food. It costs less than $20 a night. The rent-a-camp program is available at several state parks throughout Ohio.

Barkcamp State Park contains more than 1,000 acres of land and has a 117-acre stocked fishing lake. There are 176 campsites on the property available to campers on a first-come, first-served basis. There is also a 700-foot-long public beach with picnic shelters.

Barkcamp State Park   ☎
65330 Barkcamp Park Rd. · Belmont, Ohio
Handicapped access: yes

Rent-a-Camp

A POPULAR EATING PLACE

They come from three states to eat at this cafeteria on U.S. Route 40, just outside of St. Clairsville, Ohio. Mehlman's has been in business for more than three decades. Everything is made daily from scratch: fresh soups, breads, pies. They offer dozens of entrees ranging from meat loaf to baked steak. Lines of hungry customers stretch out the front door on weekends. But the line moves surprisingly fast, and usually customers wait no more than 20 or 30 minutes to reach the serving tables. Prices are moderate, and because everything is priced à la carte, you can order just what you want.

Mehlman's Cafeteria   ☎ (740) 695-1000
U.S. 40 at I-70 · St. Clairsville, Ohio
Handicapped access: yes

36 A Romantic Getaway

Every once in a while I discover a place that I don't want to share with others, a place I want to keep just to myself. This bed-and-breakfast in Cambridge, Ohio, is just such a place.

It sits on the top of a hill at the end of a long, lonely gravel road. From the outside, it's not terribly imposing. Just a pleasant, modern ranch home that is surrounded by trees and nestled at the edge of an orchard. The owners, Jim and Vicky Goudy, originally planned for it to be their retirement home. It has a barn, a spring-fed lake, lots of pasture for their horses, and privacy—lots of privacy. Their nearest neighbor is almost a mile away.

Inside, they have constructed a guest wing with three bedrooms, each with its own private bath. There is even a private entrance from the driveway to the rooms. Each room is decorated in a different style using some of the family's antiques and collectibles. Fluffy white robes are laid on the bed in each room, as is a tray of Vicky Goudy's chocolate chip cookies. At the end of the hallway is a deck that leads to an outdoor whirlpool spa and a sauna. There is a large, octagon-shaped, glassed-in family room at one end of the home that overlooks the pastures and yards. This is where you can read or just curl up and watch the grass grow from a comfortable chair.

For an additional fee, you can go fishing in their lake, take a hayride around the farm or—my favorite—have a gourmet picnic with someone you love on a secluded hilltop overlooking miles of valleys and hills. Vicky prepares the entire picnic in several lunch baskets, and they transport you and the food to the picnic area. You arrange for a time you want them to come back to get you. They leave you alone with just the birds, the clouds, and, perhaps, a few wild deer for company. In the autumn, this is one of the most beautiful spots in Ohio.

Because of the limited number of rooms, reservations are absolutely necessary.

Misty Meadow Farm Bed-and-Breakfast   ☎ (740) 439-5135
64878 Slaughter Hill Rd. • Cambridge, Ohio
Handicapped access: some small steps in house

A GLASS FACTORY

Cambridge has always been known for its glass industry and, in recent decades, for decorative glass. Perhaps its most famous product was Degenhart Glass. The manufacturer, now known as Boyd's Crystal Art Glass, continues to turn out many of its famous products and develops new ones each year. They also offer tours of their glassmaking plant, where you can watch artisans at work molding glass. There is a factory outlet store where you can buy their products.

Boyd's Crystal Art Glass   ☎ (740) 439-2077
1203 Morton Ave. · Cambridge, Ohio
Handicapped access: yes

OHIO'S BIGGEST BAKERY

This bakery claims to have the largest single store in Ohio. If it's baked, you can probably find it here, along with some of their award-winning trail bread. Their monster cookies are as big as a pizza pie, and a unique birthday cake department features two portrait artists who can duplicate a photograph with cake icing to create a birthday-cake portrait of the person being honored.

Kennedy's Cakes and Donuts, Inc.   ☎ (740) 439-2800
875 Southgate Parkway · Cambridge, Ohio
Handicapped access: yes

OUTLET STORE FOR GLASSWARE

One of West Virginia's leading glass companies also has a factory outlet store here, where you can buy factory seconds as well as some of their first-grade discontinued items. All of these can be had at a considerable savings over new merchandise in retail stores.

Fostoria Glass Outlet Store   ☎ (740) 439-3600
2311 Southgate Pkwy. · Cambridge, Ohio
Handicapped access: yes

OUTDOOR DRAMA

One of Ohio's pioneer outdoor dramas is performed here. *The Living Word*, the story of Christ and the crucifixion, is staged in an outdoor amphitheater that creates a feeling of realism as the story unfolds. While most of the cast is made up of local volunteers, the performance has been well received down through the years. The play is shown only on Thursday, Friday, and Saturday evenings during the summer months. Call for times and dates.

The Living Word Outdoor Drama   ☎ (740) 439-2761
6010 College Hill Rd. · Cambridge, Ohio
Handicapped access: yes

OHIO POWER LANDS

Ohio Power Lands is a good example of what can be done with some land that was once strip mined. Today, 350 lakes stocked with fish dot 30,000 acres of reclaimed land. Picnic areas in shaded groves overlook meadows of wildflowers. There are hiking trails and primitive camping areas open to the public. The area is also open for hunting and trapping. All of this is free; just write for information on how to obtain the free use pass.

American Electric Power ReCreation Land   ☎
American Electric Power Company
P.O. Box 328 · McConnelsville, Ohio
Handicapped access: yes

CONEY ISLAND RESTAURANT

Don't let the name fool you. The Coney Island Restaurant did start out in life as a hot-dog stand, but that was long ago, before a fire destroyed the original place. The new restaurant still sells the famous Coney Island dogs, but they have also turned it into a full-scale family restaurant that has become a favorite stop for tour groups. The place is also known for its pies, made fresh every day. While they don't offer tablecloths or six forks and four knives at every place setting, this is a good place to take the kids for some home-cooked, plentiful servings.

Theo's Restaurant   ☎ (740) 432-3878
632 Wheeling Ave. · Cambridge, Ohio
Handicapped access: yes

SOUTHWEST OHIO

37 From the Wright Brothers to the Moon

Ohio's contribution to aviation is unparalleled in the world. Not only were the Wright brothers, who first proved man could fly with a powered aircraft, born here; the Buckeye State is also the birthplace of John Glenn, first American to orbit the earth, and Neil Armstrong, the first human to walk on the moon. If a group of Dayton-area enthusiasts had their way, the motto, "Ohio, the heart of it all" would be replaced by the slogan, "Ohio, birthplace of aviation."

If you would like to see and experience what it was like to fly in the days of the Wright brothers, head down to Miamisburg, Ohio, and sign up for a flight in the "Wright B Flyer." This is as close a replica of the Wright brothers' first commercial aircraft as modern aviation regulations will allow. You sit on an open wing, just as the first army pilots did. The two propellers are driven by a single huge bicycle chain. The contraption looks more like a box kite than an airplane.

The plane was built by a group of aviation professionals who wanted to re-create the army's first aircraft in such a way that they could actually fly it. While they have substituted some modern steel rigging for the original piano wire and added a transponder and radio to keep federal officials happy, the craft still looks and flies like the original.

For a donation of $150 you can sign up to take a flight in the "Wright B Flyer." You must sign a release; then you are escorted to the aircraft and helped to a seat on the wing beside the pilot. You are offered a pair of goggles, since there is no cabin and no windshield on the plane. The two propellers are behind you. Once they fire up, conversation is very difficult. You taxi to the end of the runway and start your takeoff roll. It hardly seems that you are going fast enough when the plane gently drifts into the air.

Flying the plane, as one pilot put it, is "like driving a tractor across a freshly plowed field." The flight consists of a straight-ahead course at an altitude of about 50–75 feet for a distance of roughly a thousand feet (higher and farther than the Wright brothers flew on their first flight). Then you land and are taxied back to the hangar, where you can pose for pictures in the plane and receive a certificate that tells the world you flew in the same aircraft that taught the world to fly.

The Wright B Flyer

Weather permitting, the flights are scheduled, by reservation only, on Tuesday, Thursday, and Saturday. The hangar, which is a replica of the Wright brothers' early hangar, serves a dual purpose: storage space for the aircraft, and a museum (with a gift shop of early flight memorabilia).

Wright B Flyer, Inc.   ☎ (937) 885-2327
10550 Springboro Pike • Miamisburg, Ohio
Handicapped access: yes, to museum; steps onto airplane

THE BIRTHPLACE OF MOONWALKING

The man who made the "one small step for man, one giant leap for mankind," Neil Armstrong, first man to walk on the moon, was raised in Wapakoneta, Ohio. Today, a moon-shaped building that seems to be rising from a mound along Interstate 75 is a museum dedicated to Armstrong's history-making voyage. Inside, you will find the small airplane in which he learned to fly. There are pictures and memorabilia that trace his life from small-town Ohio to outer space. Also on display are personal items that he took with him to the moon, and there is a theater where a film of the most-watched event in history is played over and over. There is also a gallery of news headlines from around the world and copies of awards and presentations given to Armstrong on his return to earth. A dramatic place to take a photo of the family is at the end of the sidewalk leading to the museum entrance. It resembles an airport runway leading to a rising moon.

Neil Armstrong Museum   ☎ (419) 738-8811
I-75 & Bellefontaine Rd. • Wapakoneta, Ohio
Handicapped access: yes

Neil Armstrong Museum

A HALLOWEEN MUSEUM

Another little-known Dayton-area attraction, Foy's, really comes to life each September and October when this year-round costume shop expands over much of downtown Fairborn's two main city blocks. Here you will find costumes for adults and children, items you can use to make your own costumes, haunted house exhibits—mechanical or just plain scary—and even a museum dedicated to the best of the haunted house exhibits they sell. (There is a small charge to visit the museum.) You can't miss it; larger-than-life Halloween figures adorn the tops of many downtown buildings.

Foy's Variety, Halloween and Costume Stores   ☎ (937) 878-0671
20 E. Main St. • Fairborn, Ohio
Handicapped access: yes

From My Mailbag...

Dear Mr. Zurcher,

My husband and I would like To go To ThaT fanTasy hoTel you Told abouT on TV. The one ThaT had The dungeon and The cave-like rooms. Do you know if They give discounTs To senior ciTizens?

--Anxious in Bedford

38 The Adventure of Finding a Motel

On one of our first trips—to Dayton to visit the U.S. Air Force Museum—videographer Bill West and I decided to stay overnight and do some more taping the next day. Since we had no reservations, we opted to look for a nearby motel when we finished for the day.

It was almost dark when we started our search and not far from the museum we spotted a sign that said, "OTEL." The "M" had burned out.

We tried the door to the office, but it was locked. A clerk motioned us to the side of the building where there was a small window guarded by bulletproof glass and equipped with an intercom system.

A tinny voice asked if we had reservations. I replied that we didn't but were looking for two single rooms just for the night.

A metal drawer, like those in all-night gasoline stations popped out of the wall, hitting me in the stomach. Inside were two registration forms.

"That'll be forty dollars per room, each!" announced the tinny voice from the intercom.

Bill West, who had been studying the spray-painted graffiti on the walls of the motel and had pointed out an abandoned car in the parking lot, suggested at this point that perhaps we should look at one of the rooms before handing over our money.

The clerk looked slightly offended but agreed to meet us at the front door.

The three of us walked to a string of rooms located next to a large, smelly dumpster at the rear of the complex. The doors to the rooms had three dead-bolt locks each.

The clerk pulled a large ring of keys from his belt and started searching for keys to open the room. When the locks had been opened, he turned the handle but nothing happened. He finally put his shoulder against the door and gave a great push, and the door swung open.

Inside was a metal-frame bed, a small table, two mismatched chairs, and a television set that looked as though it belonged in a museum.

I walked to the bed and sat down to check the mattress. Suddenly

I found my chin nearly on my knees as the bed sagged to the floor under my weight.

"I don't think we want this room," Bill West said as he helped me up off the bed.

"No problem," the clerk replied. "I show you another one. Much better."

He led us around the corner to a side of the motel hidden from the highway. There was a chained-in area with two very surly guard dogs pacing back and forth and growling at us.

"Uh, what are the guard dogs for?" I asked.

"Oh, we keep them in the office at night to discourage holdups," the clerk replied with a smile.

He led us to another room that also had the three locks on the door. This time the door sprung open as soon as the locks were released.

This room was decorated just as plainly as the other one. I walked to the bed, but this time I did not sit down. I just leaned down and pushed on the mattress.

It was like pushing on the floor. It was as hard as a rock. As I was straightening up, I noticed several dead bugs, lying feet up, on the window sill and a few others, still living, scurrying for cover.

From the expression on Bill West's face he had seen them too. He was already headed for the door. I followed him. The clerk pursued us down the driveway.

"How 'bout I give you a better price?" the clerk said.

"No!" we both answered.

He didn't give up.

"I give you both rooms for twenty dollars a night," he urged.

"No!" we answered.

"I make it fifteen dollars a night," he said.

We just kept on walking towards our car.

"Hokay," the clerk shouted after us, "I give you my best deal: ten dollars a night!"

We drove off, the clerk still standing in the middle of the driveway.

Some hours later we finally located rooms in a large chain motel.

About three o'clock in the morning there was a roar that brought me out of a sound sleep and to my feet. I stumbled to the door and peeked out.

There in the hallway were about a dozen outlaw bikers. One of them had just won a bet that he could ride his motorcycle up the stairs and down the hall.

These days when we travel we always ask if there are any conventions going on at the motel, and we always ask to see the room before we register.

U.S. AIR FORCE MUSEUM

The largest military aviation museum in the world, this is perhaps one of Ohio's best year-round attractions. It offers a spectrum of aviation history from the Wright brothers through two world wars and Vietnam, and includes exhibits on space exploration. There is an IMAX theater that puts you right in the pilot's seat. In the 10 acres of exhibits there are more than 300 aircraft on display. My favorite spot at the museum is in the annex, located on the other side of the runway and reachable by bus from the main building. It houses many additional aircraft, including those once used by U.S. presidents. Here you will find Harry Truman's *Independence*, the *Columbine* used by Dwight Eisenhower, and planes once used by John F. Kennedy, Lyndon Johnson, and others. Several of the presidential aircraft are open, and you can walk through them and see what presidential travel was like.

One of the nicest things about the museum is that admission is free. There is a charge for the IMAX theater. Open seven days a week.

U.S. Air Force Museum ☎ (937) 255-3284
Wright-Patterson AFB
Springfield Pike • Dayton, Ohio
Handicapped access: yes

CARILLON HISTORICAL PARK

This may be one of the least-known attractions in Dayton. It is a 65-acre park hidden away near the river. Here, the Deeds Carillon, a huge bell tower that overlooks the park, is the site of concerts at various times during the year. There is also a small historical village that includes a 1905 Wright brothers plane, a replica of their bicycle shop, a 97-year-old schoolhouse, and a number of other interesting buildings and displays. The park is closed November through March. There is an admission charge.

Carillon Historical Park   ☎ (937) 293-2841
1000 Carillon Blvd. • Dayton, Ohio
Handicapped access: yes, steps into some historical buildings

DAYTON'S EARLIEST RESIDENTS

A few years ago, while excavating for a sewage disposal plant in Dayton, workers uncovered an 800-year-old farming village along the Great Miami River. Today, SunWatch has become an educational center and tourist attraction. While the village has been rebuilt by staff and volunteers, the mystery of what happened to its original Native American residents is still unsolved.

SunWatch Indian Village   ☎ (937) 268-8199
2301 W. River Rd. • Dayton, Ohio
Handicapped access: yes

THE STORY OF THE CIVIL RIGHTS MOVEMENT

At nearby Wilburforce, you can see the story of the 1960s Civil Rights movement unfold in photos, exhibits, films, and recordings. Housed here is the Afro-American Cultural Center, which, besides the permanent exhibit on the Civil Rights movement, offers constantly changing exhibits of paintings and other cultural activities.

National Afro-American Museum & Cultural Center   ☎ (937) 376-4944
1350 Brush Rd. • Wilburforce, Ohio
Handicapped access: yes

TRAPSHOOTERS HALL OF FAME

Ohio may have more halls of fame than any other state in the nation. We celebrate the very best in football, inventors, broadcasters, rock musicians, and even trapshooters.

This is a national exhibit that preserves the memory of such trapshooters as Annie Oakley and famed composer John Philip Sousa, among many others. Here you can see the guns used by the enshrinees as well as photos of trapshooting championships. The hall is open Monday through Friday.

Trapshooting Hall of Fame, Inc.   ☎ (937) 898-1945
601 W. National Rd. • Vandalia, Ohio
Handicapped access: steps to museum

39 A Most Unusual Grocery Store

No one will accuse Jim Bonaminio of being conservative in his approach to the grocery business. Take the entrance to his store in Fairfield, Ohio, just outside of Cincinnati. In the summertime, the drive is lined with palm trees. Real palm trees. And at the entrance to the store is a jungle lake, filled with life-size fiberglass pink and blue hippopotami, giraffes, and other creatures of the jungle. There is even a waterfall.

Along the walk to the front door are six-foot-tall lollipops, also made of fiberglass in various colors.

Welcome to Jungle Jim's Grocery. One of the first things you spot walking into the store is a six-foot-tall stuffed lion dressed like Elvis Presley. The animated figure bursts into one of Presley's songs every few minutes. Overlooking the checkout counter is an animated hippo playing a piano. Sometimes the clerks dress up in gorilla costumes to wait on customers.

If you see a man on roller skates rolling up and down the aisles, carrying a cap pistol and exchanging shots with stock boys one minute, helping a lady choose the freshest vegetables the next, you have just met "Jungle Jim" Bonaminio, the owner.

Jim Bonaminio grew up in Lorain County and began his career selling fruit and vegetables out of the back of his pickup truck at busy intersections. Today he is considered one of the top independent grocers in America as well as one of the most innovative.

In his store you will find an espresso coffee bar where you can have a hot cup of the flavor of the day, chosen from hundreds of coffees from around the world. He has imported foods from all parts of the globe and a wonderful bakery. He pioneered the olive bar idea for grocery stores (it's like a salad bar, but it features about a dozen different kinds of olive). His vegetable and fruit section covers nearly half the store, and most of the produce is fresh from the farm. In short, it's the kind of grocery store most of us would like to have in our neighborhood.

So why all the weirdness? Bonaminio wisely points out that kids love to come to his grocery store—and that children often influence where parents shop. He also notes that the palm trees and the waterfall help people remember and talk about his store. While some of his competitors may call Jim Bonaminio crazy, he's laughing all the way to the bank.

Open seven days a week.

Jungle Jim's Grocery   ☎ (513) 829-1919
5440 Dixie Highway · Fairfield, Ohio
Handicapped access: yes

Jungle Jim's Grocery

ABOUT THAT CINCINNATI CHILI

You can't come to Cincinnati without trying the chili for which the city is famous. Whether you have it three-way or four-way, it is a gastronomic experience. The chili, more like spaghetti with a cinnamon-flavored tomato sauce, is served with optional cheese, onions, and red beans. There are chili shops all over Cincinnati. The one we tried is perhaps the best known.

Skyline Chili   ☎ (513) 874-1188
4180 Thunderbird Lane · Fairfield, Ohio
Handicapped access: yes

A NEW USE FOR OLD TRAIN STATIONS

Cincinnati has taken the beautiful, old, but abandoned Union Terminal and made it into an outstanding tourist attraction. Today, it houses the Cincinnati History Museum, Cinergy Children's Museum, Museum of Natural History & Science, and a huge state-of-the-art OMNIMAX movie theater.

In the Museum of Natural History & Science, you can walk through a cave and a glacier. In the history wing you can stroll through Cincinnati's riverboat era; a life-size paddle-wheel boat tied at a wharf is a popular display.

The OMNIMAX theater offers a 72-foot-high domed screen that wraps above and around the viewers to give a lifelike effect to the movies.

The huge rotunda of the building has been maintained much as it was in its glory days. Massive murals still cover the walls. The old information center in the center of the rotunda today serves as a visitor relations booth for the three museums and theater. With its shops, theaters, and restaurants, the museum center has something for everyone in the family.

Cincinnati Museum Center   ☎ (800) 733-2077 or (513) 287-7000
1301 Western Ave. • Cincinnati, Ohio
Handicapped access: yes

Cincinnati Museum Center

A RIVERBOAT CRUISE

If you can't afford a cruise for a week or two on the *Delta Queen*, perhaps you can afford an afternoon on the *Belle of Cincinnati* or the *Mark Twain*, two of Cincinnati's paddle-wheel tour boats.

It's a great way to see the Cincinnati skyline and learn a bit about the history of this famous river port. They offer lunch, dinner, and Sunday brunch cruises, and full day trips.

B. B. Riverboats   ☎ (854) 261-8500
1 Madison Ave. · Covington, Kentucky
Handicapped access: yes

B. B. Riverboats

A PRESIDENT WAS BORN HERE

William Howard Taft, the 27th president of the United States, was born in Cincinnati. He was the only man ever to serve as both president of the U.S. and as chief justice of the U.S. Supreme Court.

His birthplace has been restored by the National Park Service and is open to the public. The home had for many years been an apartment house, and little was left of the original floor plan. The park service was able to restore it by using Taft's mother's letters to friends, in which she described the rooms, the wallpaper, and the furniture.

William Howard Taft National Historic Site ☎ (513) 684-3262
2038 Auburn Ave. • Cincinnati, Ohio
Handicapped access: yes

SOME BARGAIN SHOPPING

Just outside of Cincinnati is a place that manufactures down-filled comforters for some of the major department and specialty stores in America. They have an outlet store at the factory, where you can buy not only the comforters but down-filled clothing as well. The best buys are the comforter seconds, which may have been rejected by the department stores because of a crooked stitch or mismatched fabric. You can usually save up to 50 percent on these items, but you have to ask for them.

Down-Lite International ☎ (513) 489-3696
7818 Palace Dr.. • Cincinnati, Ohio
Handicapped access: yes

From My Mailbag...

Mr. Zurcher,

You were talking about a "One Tank Trip" to Canada last night on TV. Will it be about the same distance if I take my car?

--Sandusky, Ohio

40 Antique Capital of the Midwest

The tiny community of Waynesville, in Warren County, is only five city blocks long and has only one main street. Yet in those five blocks are packed nearly 40 antique shops with hundreds of antique dealers and their wares, making this community the "Antique Capital of the Midwest."

There was a Waynesville even before there was a state of Ohio. The village was founded in 1796, and many of the town's older buildings have been preserved.

The town also sponsors one of the stranger, but quite popular festivals in the state: the Ohio Sauerkraut Festival. Held for 25 years now, this festival is one of few places you'll find candy made from sauerkraut and even ice cream with a sauerkraut base!

What makes the festival stranger still is that the town is not known for raising cabbage, nor are many people here of German heritage. In fact, the idea for the festival grew out of a meeting by town merchants over ideas for a festival, and one merchant made the chance remark that he had just had sauerkraut for lunch and had enjoyed it. Why not sponsor a sauerkraut festival? They did, and the rest is pungent history.

The Village of Waynesville   ☎ (513) 897-8855 Fax: (513) 897-9833
Waynesville Area Chamber of Commerce
108 N. Main St. • Waynesville, Ohio

WHEN KNIGHTS WERE BOLD

If you have ever fantasized about living in a time of knights and dragons, lords and ladies, you can live out your fantasy here in Southwest Ohio. For nine weekends each summer, a 16th-century English country fair comes to life in the rolling hills of Warren County, complete with a 30-acre village where armored knights on horseback joust with spears and swords. There are court dancers and jesters, strolling minstrels, jugglers, and even serving wenches. Craftspeople from around the country come to the festival to sell swords, clothing, and blown-glass items, and traditional foods of the period are served.

The festival runs from late August into October on weekends.

The Ohio Renaissance Festival ☎ (513) 897-7000
S.R. 73 (2 miles west of I-71) • Harveysburg, Ohio
Handicapped access: yes

The Ohio Renaissance Festival

A REALLY BIG FLEA MARKET

On a nice summer weekend, nearly a thousand vendors can be found set up indoors and outdoors here at the intersection of I-71 and State Route 73. The permanent buildings can hold 500 dealers; hundreds more set up in the surrounding parking lots during the summer when the weather permits.

Open year round on Saturday and Sunday.

Caesar Creek Flea Market ☎ (937) 382-1669
7763 S.R. 73 West • Wilmington, Ohio
Handicapped access: limited

PARAMOUNT'S KINGS ISLAND AMUSEMENT PARK

One of America's most famous theme parks, Kings Island has more than 350 acres of thrill rides, water park, shops, and restaurants. It is home of the Beast, the world's longest wooden roller coaster; King Cobra, America's first stand-up looping roller coaster;

and the Racer, a double-track wooden coaster with one train running forward and one running backward.

WaterWorks is a 15-acre water park with 15 water slides, including inner-tube rides—guaranteed to get you very wet and cool you off on a hot Ohio summer's day.

Paramount's Kings Island Theme and Water Park   ☎ (800) 288-0808
6300 Kings Island Dr. • Kings Island, Ohio
Handicapped access: yes

A ROMANTIC HIDEAWAY

We found this tiny cottage tucked behind a historic home in Lebanon. It's owned by an artist, who hand painted all the tiles in the kitchen, bathroom, and around the gas-fired fireplace.

There is an in-ground swimming pool just outside the door, and a hot tub nearby. The cottage, built in 1864, was once a carriage house before being converted to a bed-and-breakfast. It now has a kitchen, private bath, and loft bedroom.

The Artist's Cottage Bed-and-Breakfast   ☎ (888) 233-2378
458 E. Warren St. • Lebanon, Ohio
Handicapped access: yes

ONE TANK TIP #10

Don't Be a Dim Bulb

If you like to read in bed take along a 100-watt light bulb. Many hotels and motels use small wattage bulbs as an economy measure, making reading a chore.

41 But Never on Tuesday

One of Southwest Ohio's hidden gems is the historic Clifton Mill in Clifton, Ohio. It's the largest water-powered gristmill in the world still operating. The waters of the Little Miami River are diverted through the base of the mill, powering the grinding wheel much as they have done for almost 200 years.

In addition to fresh-ground flour and meal, the mill also offers a gift shop which sells its product and other souvenirs.

There is a small restaurant where the breakfast fare is legendary. They make pancakes here—I mean they make *real* pancakes here. Pancakes that are almost the size of manhole covers. They boast that rarely can anyone finish a stack of three of their flapjacks. For dessert, if you are still hungry, they offer their signature oatmeal pie.

The mill really shines during the Christmas season. The day before Thanksgiving, they turn on more than two million lights that outline the mill, mill wheel, and adjoining valley. There is also a display of three thousand animated Santa Claus figures and a miniature model of the village of Clifton that has electric trains and even an animated Christmas parade. There is also a Santa Claus workshop where a real Santa practices for the big night every 15 minutes by running up and down his chimney and waving to appreciative families watching from below.

Not surprisingly, at Christmastime the mill attracts thousands of people each evening. A sizable staff is required to serve the crowd and to keep people from wandering too close to the illuminated mill wheel or from falling into the valley of the Little Miami River, which runs through the grounds.

The lights are on at the mill each evening, except Tuesdays, until New Year's Day. On Tuesdays, the lights are out, and the mill is closed. It says so in all their advertising. There are signs posted all around the front of the mill saying, "Closed on Tuesdays."

The first year that they lit the mill, Tony Santariano, the owner, put the lighting display on a timer, so the lights came on promptly each evening at 6:00 p.m. and off at 9:30 p.m. On Tuesdays, he would just turn off the timer so the lights would not come on.

That year, Christmas happened to fall on a Tuesday, and so the mill was closed. Christmas night, Tony and two of his daughters were moving a canoe, which they had received as a gift, from their home to a storeroom in the darkened mill. However, when they pulled up to the street the mill is on, they found it choked with cars and people. It was about 5:45 p.m. Darkness had just fallen, and people were waiting to see the lights come on.

Tony tried to explain to the crowd that there would be no lights tonight, that the mill was closed on Tuesdays, and, for safety reasons, he could not turn on the lights because he had no staff. The crowd was not happy about this. In fact they became downright surly. They started to shout at Tony and his daughters. The trio, with their canoe, beat a hasty retreat inside the mill.

"Don't turn on any lights!" Tony warned his daughters. "If they see a light on, they'll think I changed my mind and that we're open."

He told one of his daughters to toss him the mill keys. He wanted to be sure the door was locked.

She tossed the keys, which went sliding under a counter. The three were searching the floor trying to find the keys in the blacked-out room when suddenly:

"WHAM!"

The night was flooded with lights. Tony had forgotten to turn off the timer, and all the thousands of lights outside had sprung to life.

The crowd of nearly 200 outside cheered and surged forward onto the grounds. Realizing that the three of them could not control so large a crowd, Tony ran to the light switch and turned it off, plunging the mill into darkness again.

For the next half-hour Tony and his daughters huddled on the floor of the darkened mill as people pounded on the door, occasionally peeking out windows to see if the angry crowd had left.

The timer is now gone. Nowadays the lights are turned on manually, to burn Wednesday through Monday nights. But never on Tuesday. Closed on Tuesdays

The Historic Clifton Mill   ☎ (937) 767-5501
75 Water St. • Clifton, Ohio
Handicapped access: steps into mill

THE LAST REAL DAIRY

Just a short distance from Clifton is perhaps the last dairy in Ohio to serve unpasteurized milk. Young's Jersey Dairy has been in business for decades, and when the law was passed requiring all milk to be pasteurized, they and other existing dairies were exempted. What this all means is that, while their milk meets all safety and health requirements, by being non-pasteurized—some say—it is easier to digest. It has natural vitamins and some of the richest butterfat content of all milk still used in making ice cream.

In fact, Young's has become a tourist attraction. Their dairy farm is next door to the store, and the barns are open to visitors. Kids can pet baby cows and goats, climb on tractors, and watch the milking operation.

Next door in the dairy, which is open 24 hours a day, they serve dozens of flavors of rich Jersey ice cream. There is also a bakery, a gift shop, and a small restaurant.

Young's Jersey Dairy   ☎ (937) 325-0629
6880 Springfield-Xenia Rd. · Yellow Springs, Ohio
Handicapped access: yes

A COLLEGE TOWN BED AND BREAKFAST

This lovely old home near Antioch College is also within walking distance of downtown Yellow Springs. It has been made into a bed-and-breakfast that attracts many academics who are visiting the college.

Morgan House Bed-and-Breakfast   ☎ (937) 767-7509
120 W. Limestone St. · Yellow Springs, Ohio
Handicapped access: steps to upper floors

CLIFTON GORGE STATE NATURE PRESERVE

You can find more than 300 kinds of wildflowers growing here, and more than 100 species of trees. The Little Miami River has cut a 22-foot gorge through this park which, legend has it, Daniel Boone once leaped across in a bid for freedom after being captured by Native Americans. If you like to hike, there are four miles of challenging trails. The preserve is right next to John Bryan State Park

Clifton Gorge State Nature Preserve   ☎ (937) 964-8794
Jackson St. · Clifton, Ohio

Ohio Dept. of Natural Resources   ☎ (614) 265-6453
1889 Fountain Square · Columbus, Ohio

OHIO'S LARGEST OUTLET MALL

There are more than 75 stores in this outlet mall, and more are on the way. You'll find everything from name-brand jeans to fine china. As with all outlet malls, not everything is a bargain. Watch for close-outs, discontinued stock, and seconds for the best prices.

Prime Outlets at Jeffersonville I & II   ☎ (740) 948-9090
8000 Factory Shops Blvd., (I-71 & Jeffersonville exit) • Clifton, Ohio
Handicapped access: yes

ONE TANK TIP #11

Tool up for a Quicker Bath

Carry along a pair of pliers to remove water savers on faucets in motels where the bathtub takes all night to fill. Be sure you replace whatever you remove before you leave.

OTHER STATES

42 Smoky in the Mountains

Photographer John Paustian and I had set out on a One Tank Trip to the Smoky Mountains of Tennessee. We had decided to see if we really could make it all the way there on just one tank of gasoline. We topped the car's gasoline tank as we left Cleveland and started south on Interstate 71. In the trunk we had stashed a two-gallon can of gasoline, just to make sure we didn't have to walk in case our calculations were wrong.

We drove steadily, hour after hour, as counties gave way to state lines until we finally saw up ahead the magic words: Tennessee State Line. Our gasoline gauge was showing just about an eighth of a tank left. We drove on, carefully observing the 55 mph speed limit, wanting to nurse every mile, every yard, out of each drop of gasoline left. Finally we were at the Sevierville city limits. Our destination of Pigeon Forge, Tennessee, was just one mile away. We were truly going to make it on one tank.

We were congratulating each other when the car suddenly died. A quick glance at the gasoline gauge showed no movement from the needle, which rested against the "E" mark.

John, or J. P. as he liked to be called, swore under his breath.

"Better get the can out of the trunk," he said.

We were just coasting over the crest of a small hill when we spotted it at the bottom of the hill: an Esso gasoline station.

"Might as well coast down there and fuel up," J. P. said.

We slowly crested the hill, then started downward. Our newscruiser was picking up speed as the hill unrolled beneath us. We were almost at the gasoline station, and I was thinking how nice it would be to stretch my legs. Suddenly I realized we were driving right by the station.

"Hey!" I said. "What are you doing. Why don't you stop for gas?"

J. P. was hunched over the wheel, his eyes locked on something down the road.

Then I saw it, too, and started to cheer him on. Both of us were trying to use the power of concentration to urge our now-dead car the last half-mile to the sign that read: Welcome to Pigeon Forge.

We coasted closer and closer, but, at the same time, the road started to rise and our speed, already only a mile or two an hour, started to slow even further.

"No, you son-of-a-bitch!" J. P. shouted at the car. "You're not going to stop this close!"

He suddenly threw open the door, jumped out of the car, and, keeping one hand on the wheel to steer, began to push the car the last 50 feet. Realizing what he was trying to do, I did the same on my side. Gasping and pushing, we crossed the corporation line and pulled off to the side of the road. We had made it to our destination in Tennessee on one tank of gasoline.

This kind of determination made J. P. a joy to work with. But there were times his enthusiasm almost got us into trouble.

On the last morning of our stay in Tennessee, I heard a buzzing sound. I thrashed around in the predawn darkness, groping around on my nightstand for an errant alarm clock, only to realize that it was not a clock but my phone that was buzzing.

I snatched it off the stand and growled, "HELLO!"

"Good morning, it's time for magic!" J. P. answered brightly.

"What time is it?" I mumbled.

"Three a.m.," he responded.

"Three a.m.!" I shouted back. "It's the middle of the night. Have you been drinking?"

"Come on, get out of bed," he urged. "It's almost Magic Time."

"What are you talking about?" I demanded.

"I want to get up in the Smokies to see the sunrise and capture all that great magical color in the early morning," he replied. "Besides, you said you wanted to see the real Smoky Mountains, and this is your chance."

The memory of my words haunted me as I stumbled around the motel room dressing, the sting of the cool mountain morning helping to get me more awake as I crunched across the gravel parking lot, still illuminated by the moon, to our car.

A half-hour later we were starting the winding climb up the mountain roads into Great Smoky Mountain National Park. The sky was turning to gold and purple in the east as we reached a lookout on the summit and pulled over.

J. P. was nearly dancing. He was like an excited child on Christmas morning. He leaped out of the car and yelled, "Come on Zurcher! It's MAGIC TIME!"

It truly was magic as we stood, he looking through his camera and me watching, mesmerized by the rainbow of hues evolving out of the eastern sky as the first golden rim of the sun pushed up from behind the horizon. Even more beautiful was the river of white fog that drifted down the mountain valleys below us. It truly did look as though the mountains were covered with smoke.

"You only get this golden light for about a half-hour in the morning," J. P. announced. "Come on, we've got to take advantage of it."

He started packing his tripod into the trunk of the car and wrestled his camera into the front passenger seat.

"Here, you drive," he said, flipping me the keys.

We had only gone a few hundred feet when he shouted, "This isn't going to work. Stop the car!"

I slammed on the brakes, barely in time, as he stepped out the door of the still moving car. The next thing I knew, he was climbing onto the hood of the car, his back braced against the windshield.

"O.K!" he shouted. "I can see now, try to drive at a steady speed."

And so, down the mountain we came—me driving, leaning out the side window to see where I was going, J. P. sprawled across the hood and windshield, chuckling and talking to himself. "That's beautiful! That's great!"

I noticed the tan pickup truck pass us, going in the opposite direction, and the startled face of the driver, but I was too busy trying to keep the car on the winding road and worrying about J. P. falling off and being run over by his own newscruiser.

Suddenly, I heard a siren. I snapped erect and looked in the rearview mirror. Behind me was the pickup truck, which now had a blue flashing light going on top of the cab, and the ranger behind the wheel was motioning me to pull over.

"I've got a cop behind me!" I shouted out the window to J. P. "He wants me to pull over."

"Not now," J. P. hollered back. "This is a great shot. Let me finish it, keep on driving."

"He looks pretty mad!" I shouted back. "I think I better pull over."

"No! Just keep driving for another couple of minutes while I finish this shot!" J. P. yelled.

So I kept driving until we rounded another bend, and where there was a wide berm on the road, I slowed, pulled off, and stopped.

J. P. lay back on the hood to relax, still euphoric about the beauty he had just captured with his camera. The ranger, about six-feet-four of him, came marching up to my window and said, "JUST WHAT IN THEE HELL WERE YOU BOYS A-DOING?"

"It was magic, pure magic," J. P. answered, his voice still full of wonder, from the hood of the car.

"What in the hell is that boy talkin' about?" the ranger demanded of me. "Is he high on some kind of dope or somethin'?"

It took us several minutes and some identification to convince the ranger that we were indeed sober, and were just a couple of nutty journalists who had gotten carried away with the beauty of a Smoky Mountain morning.

My friend J. P., who could get so enthused about the beauty of a new day, left us a short time later, losing a valiant fight with cancer. He was only 37 years old.

There is a little less magic in the world without him.

WHAT WE FOUND BESIDE THE MOUNTAINS

Probably the other most noteworthy event in this trip was the day I flew like a bird!

Pigeon Forge, Tennessee, is located at the base of Smoky Mountain National Park and offers one of the most unusual tourist attractions in the country. It's called Flyaway.

Flyaway is a bit difficult to explain. From the outside it looks like a large grain silo. Inside is a round, tall room with a grid for a floor. Beneath the grid is a huge airplane motor and propeller that drives a wind of more than 115 miles per hour up through the floor. You don a skydiver's coverall, a helmet, and protective glasses and walk into the room with an instructor. If you do everything he tells you, you leap into the column of air and actually fly!

How long did I fly? Probably about three milliseconds. But I flew. They do require everyone who tries this sport to first sign a release and watch a film explaining safety requirements and the principles of skydiving. And first-timers go into the chamber with an experienced instructor. Can you get hurt? Absolutely. It's like any other sport; if you don't do it right, you run the risk of injury. Is it fun? You bet. There is just no ride like it on earth outside of a free fall from an airplane.

By the way, if you really don't want to fly, they do have a spiral-stairway around the cylinder where you can watch through port-holes as others fly.

Flyaway Indoor Skydiving   ☎ (423) 453-7777
3106 Parkway • Pigeon Forge, Tennessee
Handicapped access: Good question. I don't know how to rate this one. Best call first and discuss your needs with them.

Pigeon Forge Department of Tourism   ☎ (800) 251-9100
P.O. Box 1390G • Pigeon Forge, Tennessee
Handicapped access: TDD: (865) 429-7444

Flyaway Indoor Skydiving

A SECOND BRANSON?

Dolly Parton started it. She built a sort of amusement park near her hometown in the Tennessee hills, called Dollywood. When she was between gigs in California she would head home and visit, lounging on the porch of her apartment in the amusement complex and talking with park guests. Most of the entertainers in the complex were related to Dolly—sisters, aunts, uncles, cousins. A lot of people laughed at her then, but they're not laughing anymore.

Today Pigeon Forge, Tennessee, is on the brink of becoming another Branson, Missouri. Theaters bearing the names of some of the greats and near-greats of country music are joining Dollywood as they attempt to capitalize on the influx of tourists headed towards the Great Smoky Mountains.

Today along the parkway that is the main road of Pigeon Forge you will find a theater named for former Miss America and orange juice promoter Anita Bryant. There is another theater named for Louise Mandrell, sister of country great Barbara Mandrell. In all there are now a dozen theaters, ranging from Memories Theater which does a tribute to Elvis, to Elwood Smooch's Hillbilly Hoedown. Visitors to the "strip" can find everything from Broadway show tunes to the Glasgow Comedy Theater, but the king of them all is still Dollywood with 40 live shows each day, 30 rides and attractions, and 50 different craft showcases.

Louise Mandrell is one of the newcomers to Pigeon Forge. Sister of Country Legend, Barbara Mandrell, Louise developed a large following of here own in the country music world, and the opening of her theater gives her a base near her fans. She appears almost nightly during the summer.

Louise Mandrell Theater   ☎ (865) 453-6263
2046 Parkway · Pigeon Forge, Tennessee
Handicapped access: yes

43 Peace on Earth, Goodwill to All

Videographer Bob Begany and I had traveled to Charleston, West Virginia, to do a holiday season One Tank Trip segment on the West Virginia state capital and the giant sternwheeler, the *West Virginia Belle*. The idea was to get a nighttime shot of the *Belle*, all lit with holiday decorations as she sailed down the Kanawha River past the imposing state capitol building and towards downtown Charleston.

The first problem was that the boat moved faster than we had anticipated, so we appealed to one of the owners to accompany us with a walkie-talkie to a site on a college campus directly across the river from the capitol building. The walkie-talkie was for communicating with the boat's captain to slow him down a bit while we got the camera set up.

We discovered the second problem when we arrived on the campus. All of the streetlights ended at a row of buildings a hundred feet back from the river's edge, which meant the last hundred feet to the river was in total darkness—and none of us had thought to bring along a flashlight.

The boat had already gone upriver and turned for its run past the capitol by the time we found a parking place and began running through inky blackness towards the river's edge.

Across the river, the West Virginia capitol glowed in the light of the moon that was just rising over a mountain behind the building. The lights of the capitol were reflected in the water, and upriver we could see the merry lights of the approaching *West Virginia Belle*. The captain told us by radio that he was going as slowly as he could, but a strong current was carrying him towards us.

In the darkness, Begany and I fumbled to set up his tripod and mount his camera. It was so dark that everything had to be done by touch. But in minutes the camera was locked on, and the eyepiece with its tiny monitor was glowing.

It was going to be an absolutely beautiful picture. The *Belle*, with Christmas carols cascading from her loudspeakers, glided serenely down river, all aglow, towards the capitol. Begany was just starting to focus in on the ship when, suddenly, his eyepiece went black.

Renowned for his ability to curse, Begany filled the air with expletives as he grappled in the dark with the battery container on the camera. He ripped it open and reached for his spare battery in his belt. I was urging him on as the ship got closer and closer.

In his haste to replace the battery he dropped it, just as I stepped closer to see if I could help. My foot accidentally hit the falling battery, booting it away into the pitch-black night. Begany's cursing hit a new fever pitch as we both dropped to our knees and started feeling around in the grass trying to find the battery. The ship's officer, who had accompanied us, was trying to strike a cigarette lighter he had in his coat. The *Belle* was only minutes away from passing us.

"WHY ME, LORD? WHY ME?" Begany implored, as we frantically moved from spot to spot trying to feel the battery.

Suddenly I had an inspiration. I jumped to my feet and called to the ship's officer with the walkie-talkie.

"Use your radio to call the ship and ask them to hit us with their spotlight!" I yelled.

Within seconds I could see crewmen running out onto the bridge of the ship, to where the huge spotlights were mounted. The night was suddenly shattered by a blinding white light. A million-candle-power spotlight froze us on the grassy lawn, the white glare momentarily blinding both Begany and myself.

Whatever hopes we had of finding the battery and saving our shoot seemed to be gone in the flash. Fortunately, the ship's officer, anticipating the brightness of the lamp, had turned his back on it and, as the light blinded us, he scanned the ground and spotted our lost battery.

"HALLELUJAH!" shouted Begany as the man pressed the battery into his hand.

Just then the night was illuminated again, followed by a sharp explosion!

We had been so intent on watching the approaching boat that we did not notice the flashes of lightning to our rear, and as Begany scrambled to put the battery into the camera, the first drops of rain started to fall as the thunder rumbled. Within seconds it was pouring, and in the downpour we got one waterlogged shot of the *West Virginia Belle* as it sailed past the capitol building and on towards downtown. In its wake, drifting back to us from the boat, we could hear, above the rain and Begany's swearing, the words to the old carol, "Peace on earth, goodwill to men."

Sadly, the *West Virginia Belle* has since moved on to the more lucrative activity of riverboat gambling in another state, and only a much smaller tourist boat remains to give tourists that most impressive look at the West Virginia state capitol seen only from the water.

RENT A FARM

If you want to get away from it all, then rent this mountaintop farm just outside of Charleston for a weekend or a week. Owned by a Charleston attorney, the historic farmhouse has been beautifully decorated and modernized and is used for weddings, reunions, anniversaries, and other occasions. It offers total privacy. A caretaker lives in a cabin near the entrance, and while he is available in emergencies, you are usually left completely alone.

Benedict Haid Farm   ☎ (304) 346-1054
Number 8 Hale St. · Charleston, West Virginia
Handicapped access: some steps in house

ANOTHER PLACE TO PLAY THE DOGS

Charleston also has a relatively new greyhound racing track. Open year round, it offers pari-mutuel betting and a casino with electronic game machines that play poker, keno, and blackjack.

Tri-State Racetrack & Gaming Center   ☎ (304) 776-1000
1 Greyhound Dr. (off I-64) · Cross Lanes, West Virginia
Handicapped access: yes

YUGOSLAVIAN FISH STEW

I don't know why, but Charleston is famous for Yugoslavian fish stew. Rumor has it that some Yugoslavian fishermen visited here years ago and, longing for the food of their homeland, talked one of the restaurants into trying the recipe for the stew. It was so good that other customers started asking for it, and today it is still served.

General Seafood Restaurant   ☎ (304) 744-8331
18 Riverwalk Mall · S. Charleston, West Virginia
Handicapped access: yes

44 Wings over New York

One of the skills I acquired over the years, as the result of a story, was the ability to fly a sailplane. A sailplane is an aircraft that does not have a motor. It is towed into the sky by a motor-driven airplane until it reaches 2,000 feet or so, when the pilot of the sailplane pulls a lever in his cockpit, releasing the tow rope from the airplane and begins to soar like some giant bird.

There was a time when I talked so much about the joy of soaring that friends would walk the other way when they saw me coming. I was fascinated with the silence of flight without a motor. I took advantage of any and all chances to fly, and so, when One Tank Trips began, one of the first attractions I thought of to show viewers was soaring.

Videographer Jim Holloway and I had driven to Elmira, New York, the cradle of America's soaring industry. This is the hometown of the Schweizer Sailplane Company. It is also the home of the National Soaring Society museum on Harris Hill, overlooking Elmira. An airport on top of the hill offers sailplane rides and instruction, and we had made arrangements for me to take up a sleek new low-winged, high-performance sailplane with an instructor, while Jim would go aloft with the tow plane. After we had cut loose, the tow plane would fly in formation with us so Jim could photograph me at the controls of the sailplane.

The first problem was that the regular pilot was not available for the tow plane, so a retired pilot was contacted and he agreed to fill in. However, when he arrived we began to have a few doubts. He was in his eighties! He had flown during World War II. The instructor assured us that he was well qualified and pointed out that, besides, he was the only pilot available if we wanted to do the story.

While Jim had a few misgivings, he finally agreed to go with the very senior pilot. They took the door off the plane so Jim could sit in the doorway with his camera, wearing a safety belt, and do some plane-to-plane photography as we flew.

The tow rope was hooked onto our sailplane and, with a wiggle of the tail rudder, I gave the signal that I was ready for takeoff.

We taxied smoothly across the top of the hill. I was already airborne, holding my sailplane about two feet off the ground as the tow plane, still earthbound, bore on towards the end of the runway. Finally, slowly, he lifted off just before the end of the pavement. It was a good thing, because less than a hundred feet beyond the end of the runway was a cliff that dropped off into the Chemung Valley, nearly two thousand feet below.

As we climbed, the umbilical cord connecting us dragged me again and again into the turbulent wake of the plane. I was very happy when we finally reached an altitude of about 5,000 feet, and the instructor told me to disconnect the tow rope.

I pulled the lever, and as I saw the rope drop away, I pushed the stick forward slightly and started to gather speed to do some wingovers while Jim and the pilot of the plane caught up with us to start taping the action.

I noticed that they had flown back to a spot just overhead and slightly in front of me. I could see Jim, sitting in the open doorway, his legs dangling out of the plane, pointing his camera at me as I moved my stick to the right and gave it full right rudder. I tipped up on one wing and turned away from them. What I didn't see immediately was that the pilot of the tow plane had decided to stay with me, apparently forgetting that Jim was sitting in the open doorway. He performed the same maneuver, with his plane going up on one wing. The movement left Jim Holloway hanging from his belt in the doorway!

As I leveled out I looked above me and was shocked to see Jim's legs churning in empty air. He seemed to be frantically trying to climb back inside the cockpit. A few seconds later he made it, and the plane suddenly veered away and started descending towards the airport. The pilot radioed me that Jim had just informed him that he would prefer to shoot the rest of the scenes from the runway, on the ground!

National Soaring Museum ☎ (607) 734-3128
51 Soaring Hill Dr. • Elmira, New York
Handicapped access: yes

TOM AND HUCK WERE HERE

Here's a great trivia question. Were *Huckleberry Finn* and *Tom Sawyer* written by Mark Twain in Mississippi, Colorado, or Elmira, New York?

The answer may surprise you, but it was in Elmira, New York that Twain's pen brought to life the antics of Huck and Tom. This was his summer home, where he did much of his writing in an octagon-shaped gazebo on his farm. Today the gazebo is located on the campus of Elmira College and is open to the public. Twain and his family are also buried in this town.

Mark Twain Study   ☎ (607) 555-1212
1 Park Place (on campus of Elmira College) • Elmira, New York
Handicapped access: steps into gazebo

A NIGHT IN A PALACE

Paul Newman has stayed here. So have senators, opera stars, and many other celebrities. This is Geneva-on-the-Lake Resort, built to look like a 14th-century Italian palace on the edge of Lake Seneca. The inn offers beauty and tranquillity along with formal box hedges, croquet, and a swimming pool. Inside, rooms range from small suites to a grand suite that overlooks the gardens and lake and includes a living room with wood-burning fireplace, two bedrooms (one with balcony), a four-poster canopied bed, two bathrooms, and a complete kitchen. This is a top-of-the-line resort, and their prices reflect that quality, though they do offer package deals that are affordable for special occasions. For an additional fee they also have a dining room with a gourmet chef.

Geneva-on-the-Lake Resort   ☎ (800) 343-6382
1001 Lochland Rd., Rte. 14 South • Geneva, New York
Handicapped access: yes to some rooms (no elevator to upstairs)

A NON-ELECTRIC RESORT

At the opposite end of the spectrum is Pollywog Holler, a non-electric ecological resort, that can be found hidden away in the woods. The owner, a sculptor, lets other artists use his land as a place to store their sculptures. It makes for an interesting walk to the cabin. What you get for the night is a bed above a sauna. The bathroom is a privy down the lane. Another interesting feature is the well. They have pumped compressed gas into it, so you can draw a whole bucketfull of sparkling water.

The resort started out as a rustic hunting cabin, but when the owner had heart problems and decided to retire to a less stressful lifestyle, he turned it into an ecological resort.

Pollywog Holler Ecological Resort   ☎ (800) 291-9668 or (716) 268-5819
Owners Bill and Barb Castle
6242 South Rd. (off of State Rte. 244) • Belmont, New York
Handicapped access: steps to cabin, gravel trails

SPEND A NIGHT IN A LIGHTHOUSE

This is one of the more unusual places we have discovered over
the last few years. An actual working, historic lighthouse that you
can rent by the night or the week. It's at the eastern end of Lake Ontario, not far from the St. Lawrence Seaway. The lighthouse is on the
National Register of Historic Places. What you get is actually the old
lighthouse keeper's house in the base of the lighthouse. It's a bit
primitive, but it does have running water, bathroom, color television, and enough beds for about eight people. The sunsets here are
world class. Reservations far in advance are a must.

Selkirk Lighthouse   ☎ (315) 298-6688 FAX (315) 298-6685
Lighthouse Marina, 6 Lake Rd. Extension • Pulaski, New York
Handicapped access: some steps

REAL BEEF ON 'WECK

There's a restaurateur in western New York who is trying to make
a roast beef sandwich as popular nationwide as Buffalo Wings.

Charlie the Butcher and his family have been in the meat business
for several generations. Now Charlie is branching out with a restaurant, across from the Buffalo airport, where he specializes in that
distinctly western New York sandwich: beef on 'weck.

What is beef on 'weck? It's a slow-cooked round roast of beef, cut
thin and mounded on a freshly baked Kimmelweck roll. (A baker in
Buffalo by the name of Kimmelweck baked pretzel salt on top of a
Kaiser roll and renamed it after himself.)

After the beef is piled high on the Kimmelweck roll, some freshly
ground horseradish is spread on the meat and it's ready to serve. If
you have never had an authentic beef on 'weck, you have missed a
rare treat, especially the way that Charlie the Butcher prepares it.

Charlie the Butcher's Kitchen   ☎ (716) 633-8330
1065 Wehrle Dr. (at Cayuga) • Buffalo, New York
Handicapped access: yes

45 Across the Lake

There are three ways to get to Canada: fly, drive, or take the ferry. The *Pelee Islander* has been a mainstay of Lake Erie travel for years, running daily during the summer from downtown Sandusky to Pelee Island, Leamington, and Kingsville, Ontario, Canada.

Grant Zalba, former news director of WJW-TV, started out as a videographer. He and I were working together when we took our first ride on the *Pelee Islander* some years back. It turned out to be a trip I don't think either of us will ever forget.

We had gone to Canada to do a weeklong series of reports about what was on the opposite side of Lake Erie from Cleveland. In those days, we had only a limited number of radio-equipped newscruisers. It was decided that we would rent a car to drive to Canada instead of taking a company car.

Our week in Canada was enjoyable. We got to meet a lot of nice people, as well as see the sights on the northern coast of Lake Erie. One of the first stories we did was on the dock at Kingsville, Ontario, where we met a Lorain, Ohio, man waiting for the ferry. He was carrying a box containing the cremated remains of a friend. He told us the man had spent many summers on Pelee Island, and it was his last wish that his ashes be taken to the huge Canadian island and buried there. The man had no living family, and the state court was going to have him buried in an old family plot. The friend, remembering the man's wishes, appealed to the court, and so on this beautiful early summer day he was taking his friend to his final resting place in Lake Erie.

On our last evening in Erie Au, the tiny vacation community directly across from Cleveland, we filmed a pair of bagpipers from the Chatham post of the Canadian Legion standing on the rocks on the edge of Lake Erie, piping down the sun. A beautiful sight.

On the final day, we arrived in Leamington to board the *Pelee Islander* for the ride back to Sandusky. It was a hot, muggy June day. Large cumulonimbus clouds were forming in the west as the boat departed. The ship was packed with early vacationers headed for Pelee Island. Our rental car had been sandwiched between two other cars on the open part of the deck by one of the deck hands. In fact, the space was so tight that when we wanted to get something out of the car we had to crawl in and out of the open window, because there was no room to open the doors.

As the first hour passed the weather got worse. Grant and I had not paid much attention to it because we were busy doing interviews with the crew and taking footage of the passengers. A sudden bolt of lightning that struck the water only feet from the boat, and the almost immediate clap of thunder, did get our attention. We headed for the enclosed cabin on the first deck to escape the torrential downpour that followed on the heels of the thunder.

The ferryboat, although a sizable craft, began to toss and pitch as we entered the full fury of a Lake Erie thunderstorm. I had always wondered what it would be like to ride out a storm on the lake. It only took a few minutes for me to decide that I wished I was on the shore instead of on this pitching craft.

In the cabin, passengers were looking worried and pale; many were becoming seasick. Grant went to help a young mother traveling alone with two children, who were both terrified by the storm. I fought my way up the ladder to the pilothouse and found many passengers hanging on to the rails on the second deck. The crew confirmed we were in a very strong thunderstorm that was slowing our transit, but they had seen many storms on the lake and didn't appear to be worried. Reassured, I lurched out onto the second deck just in time to see what looked like a large fiery basketball strike the water and then start bouncing towards the ship. About 50 feet away it exploded like a bomb. One crew member told me that was "ball lightning." I decided to go back to the enclosed cabin on the first deck.

Through two hours of howling winds and pounding seas we pushed our way through a veritable wall of water before finally pulling into Sandusky Bay and reaching the dock. On board, the passengers were mostly a pretty damp and pale-looking lot as they filed off the boat to go through customs. We were still on deck waiting for them to bring off our car when we saw a young crew member walk over to it, open the door, and jump back as a gush of water poured out the door. The storm had nearly filled the auto with water through the window we had left open.

Grant and I sponged as much water as possible off the seats so he could drive it off the boat and through customs, where we learned we had just ridden out a storm that had spawned tornadoes damaging nearby Fremont.

The car? We couldn't turn it in for several days. We left it sitting in the sun with the doors and windows open until it dried out. The folks at Hertz did ask if we had carried some fish in the car.

THE FERRY RUN

The *Pelee Islander* is still running, but it has now been joined on some runs by the *JIIMAAN* (meaning "Big Canoe"). My only complaint about the service is that they offer no narration as you cross some of the most historic waters of Lake Erie. There isn't even a tape recording telling you where you are, or what happened in this area. Also, there is no coffee shop on the *Pelee Islander*, only some vending machines. If you can't go more than a couple of hours without a snack or a cup of coffee you might want to bring along a thermos and some sandwiches.

Ferryboat service from Sandusky to Pelee Island, Leamington, and Kingsville, Ontario Summer months only for U.S. service.

Pelee Island Transportation Company   ☎ (800) 661-2220
Departs from Jackson St. pier • Sandusky, Ohio
Handicapped access: yes

BED AND BREAKFAST

We visited a bed-and-breakfast that sits far back from the two-lane road that runs along the perimeter of Pelee Island. Built in 1875, it was once a stone farmhouse and has now been turned into a quaint place for tourists. The bathrooms are shared. Hosts Becky and Howard Strowbridge accept guests year round. There is a nice wraparound front porch with lots of easy chairs from which to watch the lake.

Stonehill Bed-and-Breakfast   ☎ (519) 724-2193
911 W. Shore Rd. • Pelee Island, Ontario, Canada
Handicapped access: limited

AN INN AND RESTAURANT

Another spot to stay on the island is at this collection of buildings on the main road. It also houses one of the better restaurants here.

Anchor & Wheel Inn   ☎ (519) 724-2195
North Bay Rd. • Pelee Island, Ontario, Canada
Handicapped access: steps into building

ISLAND PHEASANT HUNT

One of the ways the islanders make money is by attracting tourists to their annual pheasant hunt. A game farm owned by the islanders raises thousands of pheasants each year to be turned loose across the island in the autumn, when hunters from the U.S. and Canada arrive in droves, ready to spend money on food and lodging. Hunters must purchase a hunting license from the Township, which allows them to take ten birds only.

Pelee Island Pheasant Hunt   ☎ (519) 724-2931
c/o Township of Pelee, 1045 West Shore Rd. • Pelee Island, Ontario, Canada
Handicapped access: gravel paths near cages

FOR INFORMATION

For more information about places to stay and maps of the island, contact the Township of Pelee office.

Township of Pelee   ☎ (519) 724-2931
1045 West Shore Rd. • Pelee Island , Ontario, Canada

From My Mailbag...

Neil Zurcher,

I understand you were advertising about a flea market. I don't know why anyone would want to buy fleas, but I have an old cat that has plenty to spare.

--Bugged in Cleveland Heights

46 Over, Under, and Through the Falls

One of the wonders of the world, Niagara Falls, is just a One Tank Trip away. It's enough for many people to just stand and look at the falls from the many observation points on both the American and Canadian sides. But if you want to get up close and personal with the falls, there are many ways to do it. The newest, and my favorite, starts not at the falls but farther downstream in the quaint town of Niagara-on-the-Lake, Ontario, Canada. Here you will find a jet-powered boat that takes you up the Niagara River against a 30-mile-per-hour current, through some of the largest rapids in the world and into the famed Niagara whirlpool.

For starters, you have to sign a release. They have a very good safety record and have never lost a customer. They supply you with a wool sweater, a two-piece yellow rainsuit, and a lifejacket. They suggest that you bring along a change of clothes. The boat, which resembles an open triple-width speedboat, carries about 40 people on each voyage. The captain of the craft and two crew members stand behind a Plexiglas shield in the rear of the boat. Before departing you are given a short briefing about the river (one of the fastest-running rivers in the world, even faster than the famed Columbia River of the Northwest), and about the boat (powered by two jet engines, it can produce over 1,100 horsepower as it pushes against the current and can reach speeds of nearly 60 miles per hour when headed back downstream). There is also a short safety lecture (there are no safety belts in the boat; hang on to the rail in front of you and always do what the captain tells you). Then, the journey begins.

The first 10 minutes are a high-speed run through the rather placid waters of the Niagara that flow into Lake Ontario. But as the river gorge narrows, the water becomes rougher, until you round a bend and spot whitewater ahead. The area is known as Devil's Hole, and going upstream through its waves almost brings the powerful boat to a standstill. The boat finally breaks free of the rapids and races onward around another bend, and you suddenly find yourself looking up at the Spanish Aerocars that cross the whirlpool on a slender cable of steel. The whirlpool itself doesn't appear as dangerous from the boat, but the captain only takes you through one of the outer rings. In those few minutes, you get a glimpse at the upper Niagara gorge spewing thundering water into the whirlpool, which has been carved out through eons by water tumbling against the stone banks of the gorge. A few sprays of wave hitting the boat barely get you wet. You have just begun to relax when they start the run back downriver.

As you approach Devil's Hole again, you realize that the waves appear bigger from this direction. Some are as high as 20 feet, and the jet boat bores right through them. If you weren't wet before, you are now. It feels like you have run into a wall. A wall of water. The boat is flooded, but pumps quickly empty it. I was warned to keep my mouth shut on the way downriver by the captain. I didn't heed his advice and found myself spitting out great quantities of the Niagara River. After getting immersed by two or three smaller waves, we broke free of the rapids, and our speed increased as we hit calmer water.

My teeth began to chatter as the speed of the boat lowered the 80-degree summer temperature, and I found myself shivering inside my soggy sweater and rain slicker. No matter, I had just taken one of the most thrilling rides of my life and couldn't wait to do it again.

Niagara Whirlpool Jetboat Trip   ☎ (905) 468-4800
61 Melville St. • Niagara-on-the-Lake, Ontario, Canada
Handicapped access: steps into boat, no seat belts

HELICOPTER OVER THE FALLS

Another thrilling way to see Niagara Falls is from the seat of a helicopter hovering over the Horseshoe Falls. You can reserve your seat at the helicopter landing field, which is located near the famous Spanish Aerocars. This ride, like others, is seasonal and only goes when weather permits.

Niagara Helicopters Limited   ☎ (905) 357-5672
3731 Victoria Ave. • Niagara Falls, Ontario, Canada
Handicapped access: steps into aircraft

TUNNEL UNDER THE FALLS

If you want to experience the full force of the waterfalls, go behind them—at Table Rock House. Here you take an elevator down a shaft that leads behind the Horseshoe Falls. This tunnel was once used to to power giant electric generators with water from the falls . It's an awesome sight to stand in a doorway carved from stone and see the tons of water from the falls cascading in front of you.

Journey Behind the Falls   ☎ (800) 642-7275
Table Rock House, Niagara Parks Commission
Niagara Parkway (right at Horseshoe Falls) • Niagara Falls, Ontario, Canada
Handicapped access: yes

CRUISE TO THE BASE OF THE FALLS

The Maid of the Mist has been operating cruises to the very base of the falls for more than a hundred years. The boats must be built in the gorge, because the river waters are too rough to sail a ship up them. The captains operate in some of the roughest water in the world but have never had a serious accident. In fact, they are called on for rescue service when someone falls or jumps over the falls. Passengers are given plastic parkas to help keep them dry as the ships make their way to about 200 feet from the base of the thundering Horseshoe Falls. The ships only operate during late spring, summer, and early autumn.

The Maid of the Mist   ☎ (716) 284-8897
Tourist Cruises
Prospect Point Park • Niagara Falls, New York
Handicapped access: yes

From My Mailbag...

Dear Neil,

Are "One Tank Trips" only for humans, or can my dog and my mother-in-law go too?

--Separated in UnionTown

POSTSCRIPT

The Cars of One Tank Trips

Many people think the only car I have ever driven in the One Tank Trips series is the little 1959 red-and-white Nash Metropolitan. The fact is, we have only used the Nash since we purchased it in 1989.

Prior to that, we used several cars during the first 10 years of the series.

We started out in 1980 showing me driving my family car at the time, a 1978 Fort Futura two-door sedan. We quickly realized, however, that we needed some sort of signature vehicle, one that would set the series apart from other reports in the newscast. My friends Bonnie and Bill Cutcher of Brownhelm, Ohio, came to the rescue.

The Cutchers have a large collection of cars from the 1930s, '40s, and '50s; they offered to let me drive their beautiful green 1948 Chevrolet convertible in the series. We used it a few times each year for some very short trips and shot lots of extra scenes of me driving

the car. In all, we used the Chevrolet for two years until we realized that it wasn't really catching on with the viewers.

I had mentioned to Bill Cutcher that one of the first cars I owned, when I was in high school, was a tiny Bantam American, made in Butler, Pennsylvania. A few months later, Bill called me. He had just purchased a restored 1940 Bantam Hollywood Roadster. Would I like to use it in the series?

For the next several years, the little two-toned red roadster, just a bit bigger than the pedal-car I had driven at age four, became the symbol of One Tank Trips. The car became a big hit with viewers, and everyplace I went the first question I was asked was, "Where's your little car?" Problem was, we didn't own the car, and besides, its 25-horsepower motor just couldn't keep up with other traffic on interstate highways. Add to that the fact that it was virtually a museum piece and I spent most of my time while driving it worrying that something might happen to it.

I resolved to get my own special car.

Then, in 1989, I saw an ad in a car magazine for a 1959 Metropol-itan. I remembered the little car from my high school days. It had a powerful enough motor for normal highway speeds. Most importantly, the price was what I could afford. I traveled to North Canton and bought the car. At first, it  was sort of an ugly duckling—black sidewall tires, black top over a red-and-white body, paint job cracked and peeling in places. Today, after a little work, the car sports a white top, original-style white nylon tires, and a new red-and-white coat of paint. When we do take it on the road with us, we can get upwards of 30 miles per gallon and cruise at 55 miles per hour on the highway.

Because the Nash has become the signature of One Tank Trips, I've had to cut down on the number of times I drive it because I don't  want to destroy it. I hope that by driving only in good weather I can make it last and remain a familiar sight in northern Ohio for years to come.

INDEX

If you enjoyed this book, try one of these other great books about Cleveland ...

Also by Neil Zurcher:

More One Tank Trips (Book 2)
One Tank Trips Road Food (Book 3)
If you enjoyed Neil's first book of One Tank Trips, you'll love discovering hundreds more unusual nearby getaway ideas in his next two books. / $13.95 softcover (each)

Ohio Oddities / This armchair guide describes the offbeat, way out, wacky, oddball, and otherwise curious roadside attractions of the Buckeye State. / $13.95 softcover

---

Cleveland Golfer's Bible / All of Greater Cleveland's golf courses and driving ranges are described in this essential guide for any golfer. *John Tidyman* / $13.95 softcover

Bed & Breakfast Getaways from Cleveland / 80 charming small inns perfect for an easy weekend or evening away from home. *Doris Larson* / $14.95 softcover

Cleveland Fishing Guide / Best public fishing spots in Northeast Ohio, what kind of fish you'll find, and how to catch them. Directory of fishing resources. *John Barbo* / $13.95 softcover

Cleveland Family Fun / Great ideas for places to go and things to do with kids of all ages. Written by parents, for parents. *Jennifer Stoffel* / $13.95 softcover

52 Romantic Outings in Greater Cleveland / Easy-to-follow "recipes" for romance, for a lunch hour, an evening, or a full day together. *Miriam Carey* / $13.95 softcover

They Died Crawling and Other Tales
The Maniac in the Bushes
The Corpse in the Cellar
The Killer in the Attic / Four collections of gripping true tales about Cleveland crimes and disasters. Include spine-chilling photos. *John Stark Bellamy* / $13.95 softcover (each)

Cleveland Cemeteries / Meet Cleveland's most interesting "permanent" residents in these 61 outdoor history parks. *Vicki Blum Vigil* / $13.95 softcover

Whatever Happened to the "Paper Rex" Man? / Nostalgic essays and photos rekindle memories of Cleveland's near West Side neighborhood. *The May Dugan Center* / $15.95 softcover

Ghoulardi / The behind-the-scenes story of Cleveland's wildest TV legend. Rare photos, interviews, show transcripts, and Ghoulardi trivia. *Tom Feran & R. D. Heldenfels* / $17.95 softcover

Dick Goddard's Weather Guide for Northeast Ohio / Seasonal facts, folklore, storm tips, and weather wit from Cleveland's top meteorologist. / $13.95 softcover

Dick Goddard's Almanac for Northeast Ohio / A fun mix of monthly weather data, fun facts, cartoons, and entertaining essays by Dick Goddard and friends. / $9.95 softcover

Cleveland Ethnic Eats / Discover hundreds of *authentic* ethnic restaurants and markets, and taste the flavors of the world without leaving town! *Laura Taxel* / $13.95 softcover

365 Ways to Meet People in Cleveland / Friendship, romance, and networking ideas for singles, couples, and families. *Miriam Carey* / $8.95 softcover